HOW TO START YOUR OWN BUSINESS

by
Margaret C. Jasper

Oceana's Legal Almanac Series:
Law for the Layperson

Oceana Publications

Information contained in this work has been obtained by Oceana Publications from sources believed to be reliable. However, neither the Publisher nor its authors guarantee the accuracy or completeness of any information published herein, and neither the Publisher nor its authors shall be responsible for any errors, omissions or damages arising from the use of this information. This work is published with the understanding that the Publisher and its authors are supplying information, but are not attempting to render legal or other professional services. If such services are required, the assistance of an appropriate professional should be sought.

You may order this or any Oceana publication by visiting Oceana's website at http://www.oceanalaw.com

Library of Congress Control Number: 2006922577

ISBN 0-19-532154-5
ISBN 978-0-19-532154-8

Oceana's Legal Almanac Series: Law for the Layperson
ISSN 1075-7376

©2006 Oxford University Press, Inc.

Manufactured in the United States of America on acid-free paper.

To My Husband Chris

Your love and support

are my motivation and inspiration

-and-

In memory of my son, Jimmy

Table of Contents

CHAPTER 6:
EMPLOYER/EMPLOYEE RELATIONS

CHAPTER 7:
SMALL BUSINESS INSURANCE

CHAPTER 8:
BUSINESS RECORDS

CHAPTER 9:
MARKETING YOUR BUSINESS

APPENDICES

ABOUT THE AUTHOR

MARGARET C. JASPER is an attorney engaged in the general practice of law in South Salem, New York, concentrating in the areas of personal injury and entertainment law. Ms. Jasper holds a Juris Doctor degree from Pace University School of Law, White Plains, New York, is a member of the New York and Connecticut bars, and is certified to practice before the United States District Courts for the Southern and Eastern Districts of New York, the United States Court of Appeals for the Second Circuit, and the United States Supreme Court.

Ms. Jasper has been appointed to the law guardian panel for the Family Court of the State of New York, is a member of a number of professional organizations and associations, and is a New York State licensed real estate broker operating as Jasper Real Estate, in South Salem, New York.

In 2004, Ms. Jasper successfully argued a case before the New York Court of Appeals which gives mothers of babies who are stillborn due to medical negligence the right to bring a legal action and recover emotional distress damages. This successful appeal overturned a 26-year old New York case precedent, which previously prevented mothers of stillborn babies from suing their negligent medical providers.

Margaret Jasper maintains a website at http://www.JasperLawOffice.com.

Ms. Jasper is the author and general editor of the following legal almanacs:

AIDS Law
The Americans with Disabilities Act
Animal Rights Law
Auto Leasing
Bankruptcy Law for the Individual Debtor
Banks and their Customers
Becoming a Citizen

Buying and Selling Your Home
Commercial Law
Consumer Rights Law
Co-ops and Condominiums: Your Rights and Obligations As Owner
Copyright Law
Credit Cards and the Law
Custodial Rights
Dictionary of Selected Legal Terms
Drunk Driving Law
DWI, DUI and the Law
Education Law
Elder Law
Employee Rights in the Workplace
Employment Discrimination Under Title VII
Environmental Law
Estate Planning
Everyday Legal Forms
Executors and Personal Representatives: Rights and
  Responsibilities
Harassment in the Workplace
Health Care and Your Rights
Hiring Household Help and Contractors: Your Rights and Obliga-
  tions Under the Law
Home Mortgage Law Primer
Hospital Liability Law
How To Change Your Name
How To Protect Your Challenged Child
How To Start Your Own Business
Identity Theft and How To Protect Yourself
Individual Bankruptcy and Restructuring
Injured on the Job: Employee Rights, Worker's Compensation and
  Disability Insurance Law
International Adoption
Juvenile Justice and Children's Law
Labor Law
Landlord-Tenant Law
Law for the Small Business Owner
The Law of Attachment and Garnishment
The Law of Buying and Selling
The Law of Capital Punishment
The Law of Child Custody
The Law of Contracts
The Law of Debt Collection
The Law of Dispute Resolution

The Law of Immigration
The Law of Libel and Slander
The Law of Medical Malpractice
The Law of No-Fault Insurance
The Law of Obscenity and Pornography
The Law of Personal Injury
The Law of Premises Liability
The Law of Product Liability
The Law of Speech and the First Amendment
The Law of Violence Against Women
Lemon Laws
Living Together: Practical Legal Issues
Marriage and Divorce
Missing and Exploited Children: How to Protect Your Child
Motor Vehicle Law
Nursing Home Negligence
Patent Law
Prescription Drugs
Privacy and the Internet: Your Rights and Expectations Under
  the Law
Probate Law
Real Estate Law for the Homeowner and Broker
Religion and the Law
Retirement Planning
The Right to Die
Rights of Single Parents
Small Claims Court
Social Security Law
Special Education Law
Teenagers and Substance Abuse
Trademark Law
Victim's Rights Law
Welfare: Your Rights and the Law
What if It Happened to You: Violent Crimes and Victims' Rights
What if the Product Doesn't Work: Warranties & Guarantees
Workers' Compensation Law
Your Child's Legal Rights: An Overview
Your Rights in a Class Action Suit
Your Rights Under the Family and Medical Leave Act
You've Been Fired: Your Rights and Remedies

INTRODUCTION

Many people, at one time or another, dream of owning their own business, of being their own boss. Nobody likes to punch a time clock or worry about the day they may receive that dreaded pink slip. The security—or the illusion of security—of being an employee, such as receiving a regular salary and periodic salary increases, and the benefits an employee usually enjoys, e.g., medical benefits, vacation pay, and pension plans, deters most workers from pursuing their dreams. However, in these unpredictable economic times, many major corporations have gone under, leaving their faithful, long-term employees without jobs or benefits.

This turn of events has caused many people, either by choice or necessity, to use their skills and knowledge to start up their own businesses. According to the Small Business Administration, interest in owning or starting a small business has skyrocketed, and the number of part-time entrepreneurs has increased dramatically. Many of these new businesses begin at home.

Working for a weekly paycheck can never be as rewarding as the income one receives from undertaking a successful business venture. Establishing a new business is statistically very risky, but the statistics are improving, and small businesses continue to be the keystone of the U.S. economy.

This legal almanac explores all of the major aspects of establishing and managing a small business. It presents data on the demographic characteristics of small business in the United States today, and defines the various types of businesses one may choose to organize. The almanac also discusses the practical problems one may face in setting up a business, such as choosing the best location and equipment, handling the finances, and keeping proper records.

An overview of the competitive world of electronic commerce is also explored, including internet buying and selling, internet auctions, electronic payments, the international online marketplace, and privacy issues relating to online transactions. Finally, this almanac examines the employer-employee relationship, and discusses the legal obligations that arise from this relationship.

The Appendix provides sample documents, resource directories, and other pertinent information and data. The Glossary contains definitions of many of the basic legal terms used throughout the almanac.

CHAPTER 1:
DEMOGRAPHICS AND STATISTICS

IN GENERAL

The U.S. Small Business Administration defines a small business as an independent business having fewer than 500 employees. America's 25 million small businesses are crucial to the nation's economy and stability. They employ more than 50% of the private work force, generate more than half of the nation's gross domestic product, and are the principal source of new jobs in the United States economy.

SMALL BUSINESS STATISTICS

Following are some statistics demonstrating the importance of small businesses to the U.S. economy:

1. There are approximately 25 million small businesses in the United States.

2. Small businesses represent 99.7% of all employers.

3. Small businesses employ 50.1% of all private sector employees.

4. Small businesses provide 40.9% of private sales in this country.

5. Small businesses provide approximately 75% of net new jobs annually.

6. Small businesses hire a larger proportion of employees who are younger workers, older workers, and part-time workers.

7. Small businesses create more than 50% of non-farm private gross domestic product.

8. Small businesses supplied more than 23% of the total value of federal prime contracts in fiscal year 2004.

9. Small businesses produce 13 to 14 times more patents per employee than large patenting firms.

10. Small businesses are employers of 41% of high tech workers, such as scientists, engineers, and computer workers.

11. Small businesses are 54% home-based and 3% franchises.

12. Small businesses made up 97% of all identified exporters and produced 26% of the known export value in fiscal year 2002.

WOMEN-OWNED BUSINESSES

The federal government generally defines a "women-owned business" as a small business concern which is at least 51% owned by one or more women; or, in the case of any publicly owned business, at least 51% of the stock of which is owned by one or more women; and whose management and daily business operations are controlled by one or more women."

Women-owned businesses are a vital part of our nation's successful economy. According to the Service Corps of Retired Executives (SCORE), as of 2005, there were an estimated 10.1 million majority-owned, privately held, women-owned firms in the United States, employing 18.2 million people and generating $2.32 trillion in sales.

A table of the twelve cities with the largest number of women-owned businesses is set forth at Appendix 1.

Women comprise 46.6% of the U.S. labor force, and 50% of the managerial and professional specialty positions. Women have also begun to occupy positions of power within major corporations. For example, women now hold 13.6% of board seats at Fortune 500 companies, and 54 of those companies had 25% or more women directors in 2003.

Women-owned businesses outpace other small business sectors in growth, accounting for 28% of all U.S. businesses, including 775,000 new startups per year—55% of all new business startups. Between 1997 and 2002, it is estimated that the number of women-owned businesses increased by 14% nationwide, which is twice the rate of all businesses. During the same time period, the number of women-owned businesses with more than 100 employees rose by 44%. Sole proprietorships comprise 84.8% of all women-owned businesses.

Women-owned businesses participate in every industry. According to the 2002 Survey of Business Owners undertaken by the U.S. Census Bureau, and issued in January 2006 (the "SBO"), women owned and operated wholesale, retail, manufacturing, professional, technical, scientific, health care and social assistance businesses throughout the United States. Women-owned businesses continue to diversify across industries, with the fastest growth rates seen in nontraditional industries, including construction, agricultural services and transportation.

A breakdown of industries accounting for the largest receipts for women-owned business is set forth at Appendix 2.

MINORITY-OWNED BUSINESSES

The federal government generally defines a minority-owned business as a small business concern that is owned and at least 51% controlled by one or more minorities. Women are not considered minorities. Minority-owned businesses are an important part of our nation's economy, participating in many industries.

According to the Service Corps of Retired Executives (SCORE), of all businesses in the United States, 5.8% are owned by Hispanic Americans, 4.4% by Asian Americans, 4.0% by African Americans and 0.9% by American Indians. Of minority-owned businesses, 39.5% are Hispanic-owned, 30.0% Asian-owned, 27.1% African American-owned and 6.5% are American Indian-owned.

Since 1997, the number of Native American-owned businesses has jumped by 84% to 197,300. Eighty-five percent of these firms can be described as micro-enterprises. Asian and Pacific Islander-owned businesses totaled about 913,000 in 1997, employing more than 2.2 million people and generating $306.9 billion in revenues.

Of the 4,514,699 jobs in minority-owned businesses in 1997, 48.8% were in Asian-owned firms, 30.8% in Hispanic-owned firms, 15.9% in African American-owned firms and 6.6% in American Native-owned firms. Minority-owned firms had about $96 billion in payroll in 1997.

Minority Women and Small Business

Between 1997 and 2004, the number of privately-held firms owned by minority women grew by 54.6%. Meanwhile, the overall number of businesses in the United States grew by only 9% over this period. Women's business ownership is up among all groups, but the number of Hispanic (up 63.9%) and Asian owned firms (up 69.3%) has grown especially fast. Hispanic-owned businesses are up 63.9% while Asian-owned firms are up 69.3%. An estimated one in five women-owned businesses are owned by minority women, and almost 4 in 10 black-owned businesses are owned by women.

Black-Owned Businesses

The federal government generally defines a black-owned business as a business in which African-Americans own 51% or more of the stock or equity of the business

In 2002, there were 1.2 million black-owned businesses in the United States, employing more than 756,000 persons, and generating nearly

$89 billion in business revenues. These black-owned firms accounted for 5.2% of all non-farm businesses, 0.7% of their employment, and 0.4% of their receipts.

Forty-seven percent of all black-owned businesses were located in six states: New York, California, Texas, Florida, Georgia and Maryland. New York accounted for 10.8% of all black-owned firms at 129,324, with receipts of $7.5 billion or 8.5%. California was second with 9.4% or 112,873, and with receipts of almost $9.8 billion or 11%; Florida was third in the number of firms with 102,079 or 8.5%, and third in receipts with $5.7 billion or 6.5%. Georgia accounted for 7.6% of all black-owned firms at 90,461, with 6.4% of receipts or $5.7 billion.

A table of the eleven states with the largest number of black-owned businesses is set forth at Appendix 3.

In 2002, nearly four in 10 black-owned businesses operated in health care and social assistance, and other services, such as personal services, and repair and maintenance, where they owned 9.7% of all such businesses in the United States. Retail trade, and health care and social assistance accounted for 28.6% of all black-owned business revenue. Fifty-four percent of the retail trade revenue was concentrated in motor vehicle and parts dealers.

A breakdown of industries accounting for the largest receipts for black-owned business is set forth at Appendix 4.

Hispanic-Owned Businesses

The federal government generally defines a Hispanic-owned business as a business in which Hispanics own 51% or more of the stock or equity of the business.

In 2002, Hispanics owned 1.6 million non-farm businesses, employing 1.5 million persons, and generating $222 billion in business revenues. These Hispanic-owned firms accounted for 6.8% of all non-farm businesses in the United States, 1.4% of their employment and 1.0% of their receipts.

Seventy-three percent of Hispanic-owned businesses were located in four states: California, Texas, Florida and New York. California had the most Hispanic-owned firms at 427,727 or 27.2%, with receipts of $57.2 billion or 25.8%. Texas was second with 319,339 or 20.3%, and with receipts of more than $42.2 billion or 19.0%. Florida was third in number of firms with 226,727 or 17.0%, and in receipts with $40.9 billion or 18.4%. New York accounted for 10.4% of all Hispanic-owned firms, and 5.6% of receipts.

A table of the ten cities with the la
businesses is set forth at Appendix.

In 2002, 29% of Hispanic-owned
and other services, such as pe
nance, where they owned 8.
States. Retail and wholes
panic-owned business reve
nue was concentrated in
dealers.

A breakdown of industries ac
panic-owned business is set f

In 2002, 73% of Hispanic-c
Mexican Americans, or Ch
or Texas. Over 51% of Pu
York or Florida. Florida l
Cuban-owned businesses.

VETERANS AND SMALL BUSINESS

In recent years, increasing attent
neurial needs of America's veterans, pa
have sustained a disability as a result of th
the armed forces. The U.S. Small Business Administration (SBA,
ports economic empowerment for veteran entrepreneurs and provides
technical assistance to veterans and service-disabled veterans who are
interested in business ownership.

According to a the SBA Office of Advocacy, in 2003, about 22% of U.S.
veterans were either purchasing or starting a new business, or considering purchasing or starting one, and almost 72% of new veteran entrepreneurs planned to employ at least one person at the outset of their
new venture.

A table of characteristics of veterans starting or purchasing new business enterprises is set forth at Appendix 7.

In considering location, 62% of new veteran entrepreneurs planned to
initially locate their business entirely in their residence, however, more
than 67% of these prospective home-based business owners planned to
expand beyond their residence in the "foreseeable future." Almost 39%
of current veteran business owners were entirely home-based. A signif-
icantly greater proportion of service-disabled business owners had
their business operation entirely in their residence than did veteran
owners who were not service-disabled.

R 2:

S ADMINISTRATION

all Business Administration (SBA),
was actually undertaken many years
ncies. The Reconstruction Finance
2 to alleviate the financial crisis
federal lending program for all
pression.
wartime defense con-
production

Business Act of 1953, Congress created the SBA. As set forth in the Act, the intended function of the SBA was to "aid, counsel, assist and protect, insofar as is possible, the interests of small business concerns." In addition, the SBA was to ensure small businesses a "fair proportion" of government contracts and sales of surplus property.

The SBA by 1954, was already making direct business loans and guaranteeing bank loans to small businesses, while providing business owners with management and technical assistance, and business training. The SBA was also making loans to victims of natural disasters, and working to get government procurement contracts for small businesses.

Since its inception, the SBA has grown in terms of total assistance provided, and its variety of programs tailored to encourage small businesses in all areas. Nearly 20 million small businesses have received direct or indirect help from one or another of SBA program. The agency has become the government's most cost-effective instrument for economic development. The SBA continues to increase business participation by women and minorities. Since its founding, the SBA has delivered about 20 million loans, loan guarantees, contracts, counseling sessions and other forms of assistance to small businesses.

MISSION

The SBA is a federal agency that offers financing, training and advocacy for small business owners. In addition, the SBA works with thousands of lending, educational and training institutions nationwide to assist the small business owner.

The SBA also plays a major role in the government's disaster relief efforts by making low-interest recovery loans to both homeowners and businesses. The SBA has offices in every state to help America's entrepreneurs form successful small enterprises.

A national directory of the Small Business Administration offices is set forth at Appendix 8.

THE SBA ANSWER DESK

The SBA operates a telephone service for small business owners called the "SBA Answer Desk." The SBA Answer Desk is a national toll-free telephone service providing information to the public on small business problems and concerns. This service provides general information about SBA programs and other programs available to assist the small business community. The SBA Answer Desk also provides a comprehensive listing of SBA publications. SBA Business Information Assistants are available between the hours of 9:00 AM and 5:00 PM (EST). If you have questions about SBA programs, or would like information on local resource groups, you can contact the Answer Desk as follows:

SBA Answer Desk
6302 Fairview Road, Suite 300
Charlotte, North Carolina 28210
Telephone: 1-800-U-ASK-SBA (1-800-827-5722)/TTY: 704-344-6640
E-mail Address: answer desk@sba.gov
Website: www.sba.gov/answerdesk.html

SBA PROGRAMS

The Small Business Administration has a variety of programs to assist the small business owner. It offers free one-on-one counseling to help entrepreneurs and potential entrepreneurs in the areas of financing, management technology, government procurement, and other business related areas. Other available SBA programs and services include training and educational programs, advisory services, publications, and financial and contract assistance.

The SBA offers a variety of loans and financial assistance to eligible small businesses, particularly those who have been unsuccessful in acquiring outside financing. The SBA offers specialized programs for women business owners, minorities, veterans, international trade, and rural development. Private lenders make the majority of SBA business loans with partial guarantees by the SBA.

The SBA also expands access to surety bonds through guarantees on bonding for small and new contractors, including minority contractors, who otherwise would not be able to secure bid, payment, or performance bonds. In addition, the SBA monitors the federal agencies to assist small businesses in securing a percentage of federal contract awards.

The SBA offers a full range of special loan programs, including:

1. international trade loan guarantees to finance U.S. based facilities or equipment for producing goods or services for export;

2. export revolving line of credit guarantees to help businesses penetrate foreign markets;

3. small loan guarantees to help businesses needing capital of $50,000 or less;

4. small general contractor loan guarantees for small construction businesses;

5. seasonal line of credit guarantees for businesses facing seasonal business increases;

6. energy loan guarantees for businesses that make, install, sell, or service energy equipment and technology;

7. handicapped assistance loans for businesses owned by physically handicapped persons and private nonprofit organizations that employ handicapped persons and operate in their interest;

8. pollution control loan guarantees for businesses involved in pollution control and reduction; and

9. loans to veterans to begin, operate or expand a small business.

SMALL BUSINESS DEVELOPMENT CENTERS

The SBA oversees the Small Business Development Centers which provide management assistance to current and prospective small business owners. The Small Business Development Centers (SBDCs) provide a wide variety of information and guidance to individuals and small businesses. The network is a cooperative effort of the private sector, the educational community and federal, state and local governments. Assistance from an SBDC is available to anyone interested in beginning a small business for the first time, or improving or expanding an existing small business, who cannot afford the services of a private consultant.

There are 63 lead Small Business Development Centers. There is one lead SBDC in every state (Texas has four and California has six), the District of Columbia, Guam, Puerto Rico, Samoa and the U.S. Virgin Islands, and more than 1,100 service locations. The lead organization coordinates program services offered to small businesses through a network of subcenters and satellite locations in each state. Subcenters are located at colleges, universities, community colleges, vocational schools, chambers of commerce and economic development corporations.

Each center has a director, staff members, volunteers and part-time personnel. Qualified individuals recruited from professional and trade associations, the legal and banking community, academia, chambers of commerce and the Service Corps of Retired Executives (SCORE) are among those who donate their services. SBDCs also use paid consultants, consulting engineers and testing laboratories from the private sector to help clients who need specialized expertise.

SBDC services include, but are not limited to, assisting small businesses with financial, marketing, production, organization, engineering and technical problems and feasibility studies. Special SBDC programs and economic development activities include international trade assistance, technical assistance, procurement assistance, venture capital formation and rural development.

The SBDCs also make special efforts to reach minority members of socially and economically disadvantaged groups, veterans, women and the disabled. Assistance is provided to both current or potential small business owners. They also provide assistance to small businesses applying for Small Business Innovation and Research (SBIR) grants from federal agencies.

SMALL BUSINESS INVESTMENT COMPANIES

The SBA licenses, regulates, and invests in privately owned and managed Small Business Investment Companies (SBICs) across the country, in order to provide small businesses with long-term loans and venture capital. The SBIC Program is one of many financial assistance programs available through the SBA. There are over 400 licensed SBICs in operation today.

Only companies defined by SBA as "small" are eligible for SBIC financing. Generally, the SBIC Program defines a company as "small" when its net worth is $18 million or less and its average after tax net income for the prior two years does not exceed $6 million.

SBICs may not invest in the following: (i) other SBICs, (ii) finance and investment companies or finance-type leasing companies, (iii) unimproved real estate, (iv) companies with less than 51% of their assets and employees in the United States, (v) passive or casual businesses, or (vi) companies which will use the proceeds to acquire farm land. In addition, SBICs may not provide funds for a small concern whose primary business activity is deemed contrary to the public interest.

Entrepreneurs can search for active SBICs by accessing the SBIC directory on the SBA website at www.sba.gov/inv. In addition, SBIC information may be obtained from the member listing of the National Association of Small Business Investment Companies (NASBIC) at www.nasbic.org, or from the National Association of Investment Companies (NAIC) website at www.naicvc.com.

THE SERVICE CORPS OF RETIRED EXECUTIVES (SCORE)

In addition to its direct services, the SBA is partners with the Service Corps of Retired Executives (SCORE), a training and counseling service. SCORE offers free, expert advice and confidential counseling with thousands of experienced business professionals from a variety of backgrounds on virtually every aspect of business. SCORE counselors help prospective entrepreneurs work through a new idea, write a business plan and get started in business. They also help growing companies analyze opportunities, plan new strategies for growth and avoid business pitfalls.

For further information about SCORE, contact the National SCORE Office at:

Service Corps of Retired Executives (SCORE)
409 Third St., S.W., Suite 5900
Washington, DC 20024
Telephone: 1-800-634-0245

The SCORE Website

You can visit the SCORE website (www.score.org) for online business advice and links to comprehensive small business information and resources. The SCORE website has an online "Learning Center" that contains instructional articles for small businesses, as well as a "Business Toolbox" that offers online workshops and tools.

The SCORE website also contains an online template gallery that offers more than a dozen free, downloadable templates to help you with small business plans, start-up expenses, cash flow, etc. On the website, you can also sign up for SCORE's free e-Newsletters that provide new ideas and small business tips.

You can also meet with a SCORE counselor in person. The SCORE website enables you to locate and link to the website of your local SCORE branch location by inputting your zip code in the search box. Free business planning and business structure workbooks are available at the local SCORE branches.

SBA SIZE STANDARDS FOR SMALL BUSINESSES

In order to determine your eligibility for small business loans and government contracts, you must meet the Small Business Administration's size standards for small businesses. The term "size standard" describes the SBA's numerical definition of a small business. In other words, a business is considered "small" if it meets or is below an established "size standard."

Most Federal agencies reserve all of some of their programs for small businesses, such as SBA loan programs and certain designated government contracts ("set aside procurements"). With few exceptions, all Federal agencies use the SBA size standards for the purposes of determining eligibility for these programs. In addition, many other political entities, such as state and local governments, adopt the SBA size standards.

Determining Size Standard

Depending on the particular industry, the size standard is generally based on either (i) the number of employees, or (ii) the average annual revenue. The SBA has established a size standard for most industries in the economy. The most common size standards are as follows:

1. 500 employees for most manufacturing and mining industries;

2. 100 employees for all wholesale trade industries;

3. $6 million for most retail and service industries;

4. $28.5 million for most general & heavy construction industries;

5. $12 million for all special trade contractors; and

6. $750,000 for most agricultural industries.

Approximately one-fourth of industries have size standards that differ from these standards that vary from between $750,000 to $28.5 million for size standards based on average annual revenues, and from 100 to 500 employees for size standards based on number of employees.

In setting the size standards, the SBA considers the following factors:

1. industry structure analysis;

2. degree of competition;

3. average firm size;

4. startup cost;

5. entry barriers;

6. distribution of sales and employment by firm size;

7. impact of different size standard levels on the objectives of SBA programs;

8. comments from the public on notices of proposed rulemaking; and

9. any other factors that may distinguish a small business in an industry.

The Small Business Act

Section 3(a) of the Small Business Act (SBA) (Public Law 85-536) sets forth the statutory criteria for eligibility as a small business:

Sec. 3(a) (1). For the purposes of this Act, a small-business concern, including but not limited to enterprises that are engaged in the business of production of food and fiber, ranching and raising of livestock, aquaculture, and all other farming and agricultural related industries, shall be deemed to be one which is independently owned and operated and which is not dominant in its field of operation: Provided, That notwithstanding any other provision of law, an agricultural enterprise shall be deemed to be a small business concern if it (including its affiliates) has annual receipts not in excess of $500,000.

(2) ESTABLISHMENT OF SIZE STANDARDS.—

(A) IN GENERAL— In addition to the criteria specified in paragraph (1), the Administrator may specify detailed definitions or standards by which a business concern may be determined to be a small business concern for the purposes of this Act or any other Act.

(B) ADDITIONAL CRITERIA—The standards described in paragraph (1) may utilize number of employees, dollar volume of business, net worth, net income, a combination thereof, or other appropriate factors.

(C) REQUIREMENTS—Unless specifically authorized by statute, no Federal department or agency may prescribe a size standard for categorizing a business concern as a small business concern, unless such proposed size standard—

(i) is proposed after an opportunity for public notice and comment;

(ii) provides for determining—

(I) the size of a manufacturing concern as measured by the manufacturing concern's average employment based upon employment during each of the manufacturing concern's pay periods for the preceding 12 months;

(II) the size of a business concern providing services on the basis of the annual average gross receipts of the business concern over a period of not less than 3 years;

(III) the size of other business concerns on the basis of data over a period of not less than 3 years; or

(IV) other appropriate factors; and

(iii) is approved by the [SBA] Administrator.

Determining Your Eligibility as a Small Business

In order to determine whether you meet the SBA size standards, you can use the SBA's North American Industry Classification System (NAICS) Lookup service on the SBA website at: https://eweb1.sba.gov/naics/dsp_naicssearch2.cfm. Enter your business description, your NAICS Code, if known, and locate your business type in the table.

If you bid on a Federal set aside procurement, and another company is awarded the contract, you can challenge the competitor's award if you believe they do not qualify as a small business. As a small business bidder, you are considered an interested party in the process. You must file your challenge with the contracting officer in a timely manner, and set forth the alleged grounds for the challenge. The contracting officer is required to forward your challenge to the SBA who will conduct a size determination of your competitor.

Joint Ventures

For the purpose of eligibility, one small business cannot form a joint venture with another small business—e.g., to bid on a government contract—if the combined revenues or number of employees exceeds the SBA size standards for that industry.

Franchises

For the purpose of eligibility, a franchisee operating under its own ownership, its own management, and for its own profit, would not be considered "affiliated" with the franchiser or other franchisees through the franchise arrangement.

CHAPTER 3:
GETTING STARTED

PROFILE OF THE SUCCESSFUL ENTREPRENEUR

One of the first questions the potential entrepreneur asks is whether he or she can handle owning and managing a small business. It is essential that this question be answered realistically and objectively before choosing to start a business. Thoroughly and objectively evaluate your strengths and weaknesses, physical and mental capabilities, personal financial situation, and personal life. Keep in mind that running a small business can be a demanding, frustrating and time-consuming endeavor, and necessarily requires strong family support.

Since the success or demise of your business rests primarily on your shoulders, you must be determined to do everything necessary to support the business. Some personality traits that are particularly advantageous to the entrepreneur include:

- Strong drive and motivation
- The ability to get along with a variety of personalities
- Good decision-making capabilities
- Good planning and organizational skills
- Strong physical and emotional stamina

Some personality warning signs that may indicate an inability to succeed in small business are:

- Laziness
- Disorganization
- Emotional instability
- Lack of physical stamina
- Lack of motivation
- Inability to get along with others

- Indecisiveness
- Impatience
- Frustration
- Excessive dependence on others

If you have exhibited one or more of the above traits in your past endeavors, you may want to work on that aspect of your personality before investing your time and money in a small business. Consider your reasons for wanting to go into business. These may include, for example, your desire for financial independence or creative freedom.

CHOOSING THE TYPE OF BUSINESS

There are a number of factors you should take into account when choosing the type of business you want to start. You should first consider the kind of business that most interests you, and whether you are well suited for that particular type of business. Consider your experience and skills, and whether you are capable of managing the business you have chosen. One of the biggest mistakes a potential entrepreneur can make is starting a business in a field about which he or she knows nothing, and in which he or she has little or no experience.

The ideal business for the new small business owner is in an area where the person has the most experience. Although past employment in the area is not necessary, it is often the source of experience for many entrepreneurs. In the alternative, the requisite experience can be acquired as a result of a hobby or special interest.

Try to learn everything possible about the business you want to start beforehand, because too much will be at stake once you have already begun operations. If your proposed business is so multifaceted that it would be impossible or impractical for you to learn it all, then you must make sure that you bring in key personnel who have the experience and knowledge to compensate for your deficiencies.

You must also ascertain whether there are any particular legal requirements for your proposed business. For example, does your proposed business require any special licenses to operate? Are there any zoning laws that would restrict the operation of your proposed business in the area where you intend to do business?

In addition to learning every aspect of your intended business, you should also research the potential of that particular business, particularly in the area where you plan to set up shop. For example, even though you know everything there is to know about antique furniture, there may be absolutely no market for antique furniture in your area, and as a result, your business will undoubtedly fail. You should also consider your competition. What can you offer the public that other similar businesses in the area do not already provide?

CHOOSING THE BUSINESS LOCATION

Time and research should be diligently spent in choosing the proper location for your business. The location of your business is a major factor in its success or failure. The proper choice of a location for your business is governed by, among other things, the type of business you operate.

For example, if your business is a retail clothing store, you don't want it to be located in an industrial district unless you are counting on doing all of your business with factory workers on their lunch breaks. If you operate a pharmacy, you may want to choose a location near a hospital or medical group. It would be advantageous for an automobile insurance company to open shop across from the Department of Motor Vehicles.

If you plan to lease space in a shopping mall, you should investigate the competition, and make sure that the traffic patterns in the mall are advantageous to your location. You would ideally like to be located next to stores that will generate traffic for your store. For example, it may be favorable to locate a toy store next to a children's clothing store.

In addition, consider the types of services your business may require in its own operation. Locating near such businesses will reduce your own company's costs. An international shipping company may need to be located in close proximity to an airport, to avoid the expense of transporting shipments long distances and to expedite deliveries. Similarly, a law firm specializing in criminal law may want to be located near the criminal court to reduce travel time and costs.

Research the Marketplace

Before you commit to a certain location, you must do some research into the sales potential of that area, including the population and demographics. You should be able to obtain such information from the local government office. To illustrate, if you plan to open a dry cleaning service in a small town, you can use population and demographic statistics to make a ballpark estimate of the potential number of users of dry cleaning services in the area. You must then take into consideration the number of dry cleaners already operating in the town and consider the length of time they have been operating. A local dry cleaner that has been in business for 20 years, serving the same community, probably has a very loyal client base.

If your research shows that the total number of potential customers is small and that there are a number of long-standing businesses in the area similar to your intended business, your chances of succeeding in that location are slim, unless you can offer additional services. For example, you may consider supplementing your dry cleaning service with shoe repair, offering a pick-up and delivery service, or operating during nontraditional hours, if those services are not already available in the area.

In addition, you should consider whether the area will be experiencing any population growth in the near future. You may be able to get some helpful information from the local zoning commission. Investigate whether there are any plans to build additional housing developments in the community. If so, then you may be able to claim a number of newcomers to the area as your customers.

You should also make sure that the economics of the area are in line with the business you wish to open. An expensive designer boutique will not fare well in a low-income neighborhood.

Whether you are buying an existing business, or starting a new business, make sure that there are no impending changes in the area which will adversely affect your business. For example, if you plan to operate a diner near a factory in order to attract the lunchtime crowd, make sure that there are no plans for that factory to close down, leaving you without customers.

Leasing Commercial Space

After you have determined the appropriate location for your business, you must negotiate an affordable lease for that space. Some important considerations include the term of the lease, the right to renew the lease, and the monthly rent and required security deposit. Since start-up businesses are statistically risky, landlords may require advance payment of up to six months rent as security.

In addition, you should make sure that the services you are entitled to are included in the lease, such as heat, electricity, and air conditioning, and how their cost to you is computed. If your business is the type that invites customers, you must make sure that there is adequate parking, for both the customers and the employees, and that there are restroom facilities available. Generally, commercial space is leased on a price per square foot of rentable area basis. Determine the prevailing rates for similar space in buildings in the same general area, in order to establish a basis for negotiating the best rates for your space.

A sample Commercial Lease Agreement is set forth at Appendix 9.

The Right to Sublet

It would be advantageous for you to negotiate the right to sublet all or a portion of your space, particularly if you enter into a long-term lease. For example, your business may flourish and you may require a larger space much sooner than anticipated. On the other hand, you may determine that a large portion of the space you are leasing is unused. In either scenario, it would be beneficial to be able to sublet all or part of your leased space. The subtenants would have to abide by the same lease provisions you do. You must also negotiate how profits from subleasing, if any, will be distributed.

A sample Sublease Agreement is set forth at Appendix 10.

Office Layout

At the center of all businesses, there is usually a general office that oversees the operations of the business. The general office may be one small room, or it may occupy an entire building floor, depending on the size and nature of the business. Activities of the business are usually planned and coordinated in, and directives issued from, the general office. Management is usually located in the general office. Office personnel usually carry out such tasks as accounting, billing and payroll. Business records are also maintained and located in the general office.

In order to make sure the general office is run as efficiently as possible, there are certain basic requirements which should be met, such as adequate lighting, desk space and phone lines. In addition, office space should be designed for easier coordination of tasks. Employees performing similar or related tasks, such as salespersons, should be located in the same area. A space designer should be engaged to render advice on the various configurations that will best suit your needs and make efficient use out of the space.

The Home-Based Business

According to the Small Business Administration, the number of people who operate their businesses out of their homes is on the rise. According to statistics, as many as 20 percent of new small business enterprises are operated out of the owner's home.

It may come as quite a surprise to many entrepreneurs, that operating a home-based business may, in fact, be illegal under the zoning laws of many jurisdictions. Nevertheless, statutes banning home-based businesses are rarely enforced unless the business creates problems, such as excessive noise, which cause complaints to be made.

The ban on home-based businesses stems from antiquated laws concerned with the effects of dangerous or obtrusive businesses—e.g., factories in residential communities. Of course, those laws could not have contemplated the types of home-based businesses prevalent in the computer age, such as desktop publishing companies.

Before you begin your home-based business, find out how your property is zoned. If you live in an area designated as residential, as opposed to agricultural, commercial, or industrial, you must determine whether there are any restrictions or prohibitions on home-based businesses in the zoning regulations. If there are restrictions, try to adapt your business to comply with them, if at all possible. If home-based businesses are prohibited, however, you must apply for a variance or permit to operate the business.

LICENSING REQUIREMENTS

In most cases, you will need a license to conduct business legally. There may be local, county, state or federal licensing requirements, depending on the type of business you have chosen.

Local Licenses and Permits

You may need to obtain local licenses and/or permits in order to operate your business. Before signing your lease, make sure the space you plan to occupy is properly zoned for the type of business you have chosen. If not, you cannot operate your business legally in that location unless the local zoning board grants you a variance. In addition, if you are operating your business out of your home, you may need a special permit.

If you plan on remodeling the space to suit the need of your business—e.g., knock down walls or expand bathroom facilities—you may also need a building permit, therefore, you should check with the local building department before you begin renovation.

State Licenses and Permits

Depending on the business you choose, you may be required to obtain a state license. For example, a restaurant will require a liquor license to serve alcohol, and a convenience store must obtain a license to sell lottery tickets. In addition, occupations that generally require state licensing include, but are not limited to, real estate brokers and agents; security guards; private investigators; accountants; barbers; construction contractors, etc.

If your business involves selling goods, you will have to apply for a seller's permit in order to collect sales tax from your customers. The sales tax collected is then paid to the state. The amount of sales tax varies depending on the state

Federal Licenses and Permits

Businesses that are highly regulated by the government generally require federal licensing, e.g., gun shops, pharmaceutical companies, investment brokers, etc.

BUYING AN EXISTING BUSINESS

Many prospective entrepreneurs prefer buying an existing business instead of undertaking the costs and risk of investing in a start-up business. If you buy a business that already has a customer base, you can start out with a positive cash flow instead of expending the time and money needed when you start from scratch. In addition, if the business has a stable financial history, you may find it easier to obtain financing, e.g. to expand the business. The biggest drawback may be the initial purchase price of the business.

It is advisable is to engage an attorney to handle the purchase. Your attorney will generally enlist other professionals, including a business appraiser, an accountant, a banker, an insurance representative, etc., to assist in finalizing the transaction. The business appraiser and the accountant may be the same person if he or she possesses the requisite experience and training necessary to properly evaluate a business.

The transaction will generally begin with an evaluation of all of the economic aspects of the business. A thorough evaluation, conducted by an experienced business appraiser, will assist the buyer in making an informed decision concerning his or her potential success in operating the particular business. The evaluation also assists the seller in setting a fair and realistic purchase price for the business.

The buyer should consider such factors as his or her experience in the field, the demand for the product or service offered by the business, the failure rate of similar businesses; the existence of competitive businesses, particularly those located in the same area, the cost of operation, and the buyer's ability to keep afloat until the business starts to turn a profit.

In order to reach a fair price, you must determine how much the business is actually worth. Therefore, you must examine the seller's financial records, including but not limited to the seller's profit and loss records, balance sheet, deposit receipts, utility costs, and supplier costs, to assist you in assessing the value of the business and making a good offer that will provide you with your desired rate of return. An accountant may be hired to investigate the company's financial condition.

Your attorney will review all of the organizational documents of the business. Depending on the type of business you are purchasing (e.g., corporation or partnership), such documents may include the partnership agreement, certificate of incorporation and bylaws, and any related documents. In addition, the attorney will review the deed and title, and related documents, to confirm ownership and ascertain any potential problems or limitations on the transfer.

Other important aspects of the business which the attorney will review and investigate may include: the lease and zoning regulations, particularly if the location of the business is a primary asset; the legal department files to ascertain the existence of any pending or potential lawsuits; the proper registration of the business name and any trademarks; personnel matters, including the existence of employment contracts, retirement plans, union agreements, etc.; and any other information useful in determining the viability of the business.

Be particularly aware of any potential problems that will affect the location of the business, particularly if the seller appears anxious to finalize the transaction. For example, if you are considering the purchase of a profitable diner that has the lunchtime crowd of the local factory as its main customer base, make sure that the factory has not made any plans to close its doors. Many businesses are sold while they are still showing a profit after the owner discovers an impending change in the area that will adversely affect the business.

After a value has been placed on the business, the parties negotiate the terms of the deal. The attorney for one of the parties will then prepare an agreement to purchase the business, which is reviewed by all parties and finalized after all of the points have been discussed and agreed upon. Once the agreement is finalized, the parties to the sale will execute it, and the buyer will obtain the financing necessary to complete the sale. The final step in the transfer of a business is the closing, when the purchaser pays the agreed upon purchase price and receives the transfer documents and business records.

In searching for your ideal business opportunity, you may confront individuals who will encourage you to participate in a particular type of business venture, generally requiring you to make an initial investment or pay a substantial fee. The types of business ventures that may be offered include franchises and distributorships.

Although some of these business opportunities may be legitimate, many are not. Their lure is usually a promise of huge profits, guaranteed sales, and extensive company support. Unfortunately, their only "business" is to take your money and run. When confronted with such an opportunity, you must investigate all aspects of the business venture offered, and the company offering it, before you hand over any money or sign any contracts. If the company is not legitimate, you will probably not be able to get your money back by the time you discover the fraud.

There are certain preliminary warning signs which should alert you to the possibility of a business opportunity fraud scheme. For example, if the individual is reluctant to put the terms of the offer down in writing, that is a cause for concern. If you are being rushed into making the deal, and discouraged from seeking legal advice, you should be wary. You may be told that the offer will only be available for a very short period. Resist such pressure tactics, and seek professional advice.

You should ask to see all pertinent company documents, such as the company's track record, including its financial statements for the past several years and a list of the officers and directors of the company. You should also request references, particularly from other investors. Make your own inquiries. Call the Better Business Bureau, and consult your banker and investment advisor.

If you do invest in a business venture and find that the company's promises to you are not being fulfilled and that you cannot get any cooperation, contact your local law enforcement authorities and complain. Even if it is too late for you to recover your investment, you will assist in protecting others from being victimized by the same individuals.

BUYING A FRANCHISE

Another alternative to starting a new business is to purchase a franchise. In general, a franchise sells the goods and services of a franchisor—i.e., the owner of a recognizable trademark or trade name, e.g., McDonalds. The franchisor usually provides training, marketing plans, supplies, and ongoing support to the franchisee. The franchisor may also assist the franchisee with finding a suitable site for the franchise, and financing for the business. The primary difference between going into business for yourself and purchasing a franchise is the loss of absolute control over your business, and the fees that must be paid to the franchisor.

If you decide to buy a franchise, you should review any available financial records of the franchisor, including the profit and loss statements and financial statement. You should also find out whether or not the franchisor is involved in any pending litigation. It is also advisable to visit existing franchises and speak with the franchise owners. You may be able to get some insight into their dealings with the franchisor, and any problems that they may have experienced.

OFFICE EQUIPMENT AND TECHNOLOGY

Every business, big or small, requires certain equipment to operate efficiently and cut down on the expense of using outside services. Technological advances have made certain types of equipment, such as computers and photocopiers, available to small business owners, whereas such items were previously cost prohibitive. Many items now have multiple uses, such as the all-in-one printer/scanner/fax/copier machines. This multi-use capability can reduce the initial cost of essential office equipment.

Telephone Equipment

Efficient communication is essential in operating a successful business. There is a broad range of telephone systems available, each with their own capabilities. The size and nature of your business largely determines the type of telephone system you require to efficiently operate your business. For example, a small, two-person, two-desk office, may not need any more than a two-line telephone system, with one unit for each desk and voice mail capabilities.

A larger business, particularly one which entails sales and marketing, or other heavy telephone usage needs, will require a more complex system. Where inter-office communication is frequent, a system with intercom capabilities can be utilized.

In addition, depending on your location, there are many services available through the local telephone company which may prove useful in operating your business, such as voice mail service, three-way calling, call forwarding, call waiting, caller identification and call return. Check with your local telephone company to find out what services are available in your area.

In any event, since telephone service can become a major company expense, you should devise a telephone use policy to cut down on personal, customer, and long-distance calls. For example, consider installing security devices for efficient monitoring and prevention.

Facsimile Machine

Another technological advance is the facsimile machine. A facsimile machine makes it possible to send and receive all types of printed material electronically, using the telephone lines. The faxed material reaches its destination instantaneously, a significant advantage for many businesses.

The facsimile machine is connected to the phone line jack. It may have its own assigned number and line, or it may share a telephone line. If it shares a telephone line, it may be switched on when a facsimile transmission is being sent, or it may automatically receive faxes after a certain number of rings. A device known as a phone/fax switch allows the facsimile machine to determine whether the incoming signal is a caller or a fax. If it is a fax, the machine will respond.

Photocopier

No matter what type of business you operate, there is usually a need to make photocopies of documents, pictures, checks, invoices, and letters, etc. Copiers can range from small, inexpensive desktop models to larger, more complex machines. Once you have determined the copying requirements of your business, you should find a copier that can meet those needs in the most cost efficient manner. You should take into consideration the purchase price of the copier as well as the cost of processing a copy, including the price of copier cartridges, paper, and the electricity used by the copier.

If your need for copying is infrequent, it may be cost-effective to spend less for the initial purchase of the copier, even though the copy processing cost may be relatively high. Printers and fax machines often have copier capabilities, in which case you will not need to purchase a separate copier, as long as the type and quality of the copies made using that machine are sufficient for your needs.

Businesses in which duplicating is a major, frequent undertaking may be better off in the long run buying a more expensive copier with a low per copy processing cost. In the alternative, leasing may be a more cost-effective solution.

Computer System

Every business, small and large, gathers and processes information of some kind. For example, a grocery store owner gathers information on existing inventory to determine what is needed to order from suppliers. Computerized scanners have largely replaced the cash register. A medical office needs to keep appointment, billing, and patient information on file.

Before computer technology became available and affordable to the small business owner, this type of record keeping was necessarily done by hand—and preserved on paper—a time-consuming and unreliable method. The computer age has changed the way small companies manage information and has helped to level the playing field.

Selecting a Computer System

Computer technology advances at a rapid pace. No sooner do you learn how to operate your computer than it is rendered obsolete by an even more efficient unit. Therefore, where cost is a factor, it is important to purchase a computer that will serve all of the foreseeable needs of your company. Before you purchase your computer, you should determine the future needs of your business, including all possible uses of a computer system for your company as it presently exists, and as it may develop and expand.

Engage the assistance of a professional with whom you can discuss your business requirements and who can advise and assist you in purchasing computer hardware and software. If you are not particularly knowledgeable about computers, you may want to purchase a system that is relatively simple to understand and use.

Desktop

A desktop computer is the most common type of computer used in an office setting. Depending on the model, components generally consist of a central processing unit (CPU), a monitor, a CD/DVD drive, and USB ports that are used to plug in accessories, such as the keyboard, mouse and printer. Good quality inkjet printers are available at minimal cost. Laser printers cost more up front but are less expensive over the long term.

Laptop

A laptop computer has similar capabilities as a desktop with portability as its key feature. The downside is that you cannot print from the laptop unless you plug your laptop into a printer. A laptop runs on an internal battery, therefore, the laptop must be plugged into an electrical outlet to recharge the battery once it has exhausted its charge. If your laptop has wireless capability, you can access the Internet without plugging into a telephone line. Although laptops are generally more expensive than desktops, they are worth it if your business involves travel.

Computer Software

There is software available that covers almost every aspect of business operations, including billing, accounting, payroll, inventory, and scheduling. Many computers include software packages bundled into the system. At a minimum, a small business should purchase software that performs word processing, basic accounting, spreadsheets, and presentations.

Before you purchase your computer hardware, review the available software for the different computer models. If you discover software packages that are particularly suited to your company's operations, you should make sure you purchase the proper hardware necessary to run that software. In addition, the experienced computer programmer can create custom-made programs in case certain information processing unique to your business is not available in commercial software.

Internet Access

In order to access the Internet, you need a computer and an Internet Service Provider (ISP). ISPs vary in the services provided and the costs assessed. There are many ISPs, all of which provide e-mail capability. One of the most popular ISPs is America Online, which is quite comprehensive in the features it offers and services it provides. The user is charged a monthly fee by the ISP for the service.

It is preferable to arrange for a high-speed Internet connection instead of dial-up, which is unreliable and slow. Many websites provide the visitor with a wealth of useful information on almost any topic you can imagine, and contain helpful tools and resources for prospective entrepreneurs.

For example, the Small Business Administration provides an online information service to small business owners, known as SBA On-Line. SBA On-Line provides information concerning starting and managing small businesses, including business advice, financing and marketing information, training materials, as well as recent news and laws concerning the small business owner.

The Internet is commonly used by small businesses in insurance agencies, law firms and in other service sectors. E-mail and research—e.g., finding new customers—continue to be some of the most popular uses of the Internet by small businesses. In addition, many small businesses are now using e-commerce to sell their goods and services online, as further discussed in Chapter 9 of this almanac.

CHAPTER 4:
STRUCTURING YOUR BUSINESS

CHOOSING THE TYPE OF BUSINESS ORGANIZATION

One of the first tasks you will undertake when you decide to go into business for yourself will be selecting the type of business organization you will form. There are three basic types of business formations that are most commonly used by small businesses: (i) sole proprietorship; (ii) partnership; and (iii) corporation.

The type of business you form will affect the way in which you must operate your business, therefore, you should consider the restrictions and limitations of each before making your decision. In making a choice, you must envision the size and nature of the business you want to build. You should also take into account the advantages and disadvantages of the different types of ownership, including the amount of control you want to be able to exercise over the business; as well as tax and liability implications.

Nevertheless, you are not obligated to maintain the same business formation and, if your needs change, you can change the way your business is structured. For example, if you start out as a sole proprietorship, but need additional funding, or someone who can contribute additional management skills, you may want to bring in a partner.

The Sole Proprietorship

The sole proprietorship is an unincorporated business, owned and operated by one individual—the owner. It is the simplest and most common business organization, and the least expensive of the three basic forms of doing business. The owner owns all of the assets and profits, and undertakes all of the risks of the business. Most small businesses start out as sole proprietorships. The sole proprietorship is owned and operated by one person—the sole proprietor—and continues until his or her death or retirement.

The Business Name

The sole proprietorship may be operated in the individual's personal name, or under an assumed business name, also known as a DBA ("doing business as"). Sole proprietors operating their businesses under fictitious or assumed names are generally required to file a business certificate with the appropriate government office in the county where the business is physically located. There is usually a nominal registration fee.

The county clerk will conduct a name search for the chosen name to determine if it is already being used by another business. If so, then another business name must be chosen. You may also be required to publish the business name in a local paper for a specified number of days to provide notice to the public of the assumed name.

The assumed name must not be misleading, and must not constitute unfair competition or trademark infringement. If so, the aggrieved party may petition the court to enjoin use of the name. It is advisable to file a business certificate for a number of reasons. For example, once you have registered your DBA, the business name legally belongs to you. Other businesses are prevented from using the same name within your state. If you don't register your DBA, another similar business will not know that you exist and may take the name, causing confusion.

In addition, registering your DBA will allow you to open a bank account in the name of your business, and you will be able to accept checks payable to your business name. Most banks will not open a bank account in a business name without proof of DBA registration. You will also be able to enforce contracts you sign under your business name.

A sample Business Certificate is set forth in the Appendix 11.

Although not legally required, it is also advisable to register your business name as a trademark in case another business tries to use your name, or a name that is likely to be confused with your business name.

Personal Liability

Unlike a corporation, the sole proprietorship does not afford the owner any protection from the debts and liabilities of the business. All liabilities are personal liabilities. For example, if the business incurs debts, the business creditor can go after the owner's personal assets to recover the debt. In addition, the sole proprietor has absolute authority over all business decisions; however, he or she is also personally liable for all of his or her own acts, as well as all acts of employees committed within the scope of their employment.

Taxation

The sole proprietorship itself does not pay any taxes. The sole proprietor retains the profits of the business. The income and expenses from the business are shown on IRS Schedule C, which is made part of the business owner's personal income tax returns. If Schedule C shows that the business earned a profit, that amount is added to all other income the individual earned that year from whatever source. On the other hand, if the business shows a loss, that amount is deducted, thereby reducing the total income subject to taxation. Nevertheless, a sole proprietor is required to pay self-employment tax for Social Security coverage.

The Partnership

A partnership occurs when two or more persons agree to form a business, each generally making a contribution to the venture, such as money, property or services, with the intention of sharing the profits and losses from the business. Since a corporation is a legal person, it may be a member of a partnership if such membership is in furtherance of the corporation's purpose. The partnership name may consist of the names of the partners or, as with a sole proprietorship, the partnership name may be an assumed name. Partners are responsible for the other partner's business actions, as well as their own.

The Partnership Agreement

The partners generally enter into a written partnership agreement that spells out all of the rights and responsibilities of each partner. A partnership may also arise out of an oral agreement, although such an agreement would be difficult to prove, thus a written partnership agreement is always recommended.

A well-drafted partnership agreement should include the following:

1. Type of business.
2. Amount of equity invested by each partner.
3. Division of profit or loss.
4. Partners' compensation.
5. Distribution of assets on dissolution.
6. Duration of partnership.
7. Provisions for changes or dissolving the partnership.
8. Dispute settlement clause.
9. Restrictions of authority and expenditures.

A sample Partnership Agreement is set forth at Appendix 12.

Taxation

Although a partnership does not pay any tax, it must file an information return setting forth the profits and losses of the partnership. The profits and losses of the partnership flow through to the individual partners. The individual partners must report their shares of the partnership profits or losses on their personal income taxes, in much the same manner as the sole proprietor. Unless the partnership agreement provides otherwise, partners generally share profits equally, and share losses in the same proportion as profits. In addition, each partner is also required to pay self-employment tax for Social Security coverage.

General and Limited Partnerships

The two basic types of partnerships are the general partnership and the limited partnership. In a general partnership, all of the partners—known as general partners—share fully in the profits, losses and management of the company. In addition, each partner has unlimited personal liability. When the partnership is dissolved, the partnership assets are divided among the individual partners pursuant to the terms of the partnership agreement.

A limited partnership consists of one or more general partners, who manage the business and are personally liable for partnership debts, and one or more limited partners, who contribute capital and share in profits, but take no part in running the business and are not liable for the debts of the partnership beyond their capital contributions.

The advantage of a limited partnership over a general partnership is the limited liability afforded the limited partners, as long as the limited partner does not take an active role in managing the business.

Joint Venture

A joint venture acts like a general partnership, but is in business for a limited period of time, or to undertake a single project. If the partners in a joint venture continue their activities, they will likely be recognized as an ongoing partnership, and will have to file as a partnership, and distribute partnership assets upon dissolution of the entity, as discussed above.

The Corporation

A corporation is a unique legal entity, separate and apart from its owners, created under the authority of the laws of the state in which it conducts business. The owners of a corporation are its shareholders. The shareholders elect a board of directors to oversee the major policies and decisions. The corporation has a life of its own and does not dissolve when ownership changes.

Control

Control of a corporation depends on stock ownership. In forming a corporation, prospective shareholders exchange money, property, or a combination of both, in return for the corporation's capital stock. Persons with the largest stock ownership, not the total number of shareholders, control the corporation and make policy decisions.

Control is exercised through regular board of directors' meetings and annual stockholders' meetings. Records must be kept to document decisions made by the board of directors. Small, closely held corporations can operate more informally, but record keeping cannot be eliminated entirely.

A corporation may be public or private. A public corporation is a governmental agency created by the state, such as a school district, city, town, or county. Common usage also refers to business corporations as either public or private. A public business corporation refers to one that trades its shares to and among the general public, as opposed to a private business corporation, also known as a close corporation, whose shares are not publicly traded. This almanac is concerned with the formation of a private business corporation.

Limited Liability

Incorporation has some advantages over the sole proprietorship and partnership forms of doing business. For example, incorporation may provide limited liability for the shareholders. Thus, if the corporation enters into a contract for the purchase of goods, and it breaches the contract and does not pay for those goods, the creditor can only enforce a judgment against the assets of the corporation. The assets of the shareholders and officers cannot be touched.

There are some exceptions to the limited liability feature of incorporation. For example, creditors of closely held corporations will likely require a personal guarantee from one or more of the shareholders or officers before extending credit to the corporation. The person who gives that guarantee will be personally liable for that particular corporate debt should the corporation fail to pay.

Piercing the Corporate Veil

If the shareholders do not operate the corporation as a separate and distinct entity, with all the legal formalities, a court may conclude that the business is not a true corporate entity and the court may "pierce the corporate veil." When this happens, personal liability may be imposed on the shareholders. This could occur, for example, where the shareholders commingle corporate and personal funds or do not maintain the proper corporate records. Further, officers of a corporation can be liable to stockholders for improper actions.

In addition, particularly in states where corporations are required to maintain a minimum amount of capital as a condition of doing business, courts will pierce the corporate veil if they determine that the corporation is not adequately capitalized.

The Corporate Name

When setting up your corporation, you must select a corporate name. This is the only name under which the corporation can legally do business. The proposed name must be cleared with the designated governmental office, such as the office of the Secretary of State. If the name you choose is the same as, or substantially similar to, that of another corporation conducting business in the state, the name will be rejected and you will have to submit another name for your corporation.

The Certificate of Incorporation

The corporation is formed by filing a certificate of incorporation, also known as articles of incorporation, with the designated governmental office of the state, such as the office of the Secretary of State. Each state sets its own fees that must accompany the filing. The filing date of the certificate is generally the official date that the corporation is deemed to be in existence.

A sample Certificate of Incorporation is set forth at Appendix 13.

After the certificate is filed, there are certain formalities which must occur. Often, in small, closely held corporations, the organization meeting, first meeting of the board of directors, and first meeting of the shareholders are held on the same day, scheduled one after the other. Stock is usually issued at the organization meeting. Adoption of the corporate bylaws, which set forth basic information about the corporation, and election of the board of directors, occurs at the first meeting of the shareholders.

The board of directors manages the business of the corporation and establishes corporate policy. At the first meeting of the board of directors, the corporate officers are elected. The officers carry out the day-to-day business of the corporation, pursuant to the policy established by the board of directors.

The shareholders, directors, and officers may be one and the same, which is often the case in a small business. Generally, there cannot be less than three directors unless there are less than three shareholders, in which case the number of directors must at least equal the number of shareholders (e.g., one shareholder only requires one director).

Domestic and Foreign Corporations

If you incorporate in the state in which you plan to conduct all or most of your business, the corporation is known as a domestic corporation in that state, and the law of that state governs the internal affairs of the corporation. If you choose to incorporate your business in a state other than, or in addition to, the states in which you will be conducting your business, your corporation will be known as a foreign corporation in any other states in which you conduct business. In addition to the taxes and regulations of its own state of incorporation, a foreign corporation will be subject to additional taxes, fees, and regulations in the states in which it does business and is not incorporated.

Because there is no automatic right to conduct business in a state other than the state of incorporation, a corporation must first apply for authorization to do business in other states. It is best to incorporate in the state in which you will be conducting business unless, despite the additional expense, there is a good reason to incorporate elsewhere, e.g., another state's corporate law is more advantageous to your business. For example, since the state of Delaware's laws are particularly favorable towards corporations, many of the largest U.S. corporations are incorporated in Delaware. However, most of those advantages are not particularly applicable to the small business.

Corporate Taxation

The "C" Corporation

The standard corporation—known as a "C" corporation—unlike a sole proprietorship or partnership, files a corporate tax return that shows the corporation's income, which is subject to taxation by the corporation. A corporation generally takes the same deductions as a sole proprietorship to figure its taxable income. A corporation can also take special deductions.

Income received by the owner of the corporation, as a shareholder/employee, which may be in the form of salary, dividend, or interest income, is taxable to the individual and reported on his or her personal income tax returns. However, shareholders cannot deduct any loss of the corporation.

When the corporation pays out salaries or interest, just as any other corporate expenses, these items are deductible, as long as the salary is reasonably related to the value of the services rendered. To avoid salaries being deemed unreasonable, you can compare them with salaries paid by other companies for similar positions.

In addition, salary payments should remain consistent. If salaries fluctuate from year to year depending on how the business is doing, the Internal Revenue Service may determine that a certain portion of the payments were actually dividends, and not salaries. This is important because dividends are subject to corporate tax, as well as taxable to the stockholder on his or her personal income tax returns. This results in a double taxation of the same funds because the corporation's profit is taxed to the corporation when earned, and then taxed to the shareholders if distributed as dividends.

The Subchapter "S" Corporation

In order to avoid this double tax, some corporations elect, for tax purposes, what is known as S corporation status under Subchapter S, Section 1362 of the Internal Revenue Code. An S corporation files an information return instead of a regular corporate return, and does not pay taxes on the income of the corporation. The corporate income and losses are passed through, on a pro-rata basis, to the shareholders, who report their shares of the income or losses on their personal income tax returns, much like a partnership.

In order to elect S corporation status, the corporation must meet certain statutory requirements. For example, among other requirements, an S corporation must be a domestic corporation that is not a member of an affiliated group of corporations; it cannot have more than 35 shareholders (a husband and wife may be counted as one shareholder); and the shareholders must be individuals, estates, or certain trusts, and cannot be nonresident aliens. In addition, there can only be one class of stock.

Once S corporation status is elected, it continues until revoked. Therefore, you can maintain an S corporation as long as this arrangement benefits you, assuming you continue to meet the statutory requirements.

The Professional Corporation

In most states, professionals—such as accountants, doctors, lawyers, and dentists—are permitted to form a corporation. Shareholders must be duly licensed in the profession. Many professional corporations are formed to allow the shareholders to take advantage of the tax benefits of incorporation. The shareholders of a professional corporation also enjoy limited liability for all claims except in the case of professional malpractice. If a shareholder commits an act of professional malpractice, he or she is personally liable.

Section 1244 Stock

If stock issued by a corporation meets certain legal requirements set forth in Section 1244 of the Internal Revenue Code, the Board of Directors may designate stock as Section 1244 stock. The advantage of Section 1244 stock is that it allows the shareholder to claim any losses on his or her stock investment, up to a specified maximum—presently $50,000—as an ordinary loss instead of a capital loss.

The distinction between ordinary and capital loss is that ordinary losses are fully deductible from ordinary income whereas capital losses, while fully deductible from capital gains, if any, are only partially deductible from ordinary income.

A sample Section 1244 Stock Resolution is set forth at Appendix 14.

The Limited Liability Company

The Limited Liability Company (LLC) has features of both a partnership and a corporation. For tax purposes, it is treated like a partnership. An LLC may have one or more owners. The owners of an LLC are called "members," and may include other LLCs, corporations and individuals. Certain types of business cannot form an LLC, such as an insurance company, a bank, and a nonprofit organization.

The profits and losses of the LLC are distributed to the owners and investors, and reported on their personal income tax returns. However, the LLC has the added advantage of the limited personal liability enjoyed by the corporation. This is a particularly attractive feature for the small business owner, who may be concerned about the unlimited liability of a sole proprietorship. In fact, this threat of personal exposure deters many potential entrepreneurs from starting new businesses.

Although the S corporation operates in much the same way as an LLC—i.e., it limits personal liability and is taxed like a partnership—the S corporation is much more complex and subject to many more restrictions than the LLC. For example, whereas the S corporation limits membership to individuals, estates and certain trusts, which can total no more than 35, the LLC is more flexible, allowing corporations, partnerships, charitable organizations, pension plans, nonresident aliens and other trusts to participate. In addition, the LLC may offer more than just one class of stock, unlike the S corporation.

The other two forms of business organization that protect personal assets from exposure—the regular corporation and the limited partnership—each have their drawbacks. As discussed above, the regular corporation involves double taxation of dividend income, and the limited partnership runs the risk of reclassification as a general partnership if the limited partner is determined to have taken an active part in managing the business.

Nevertheless, the LLC is not for everyone. The LLC restricts the transferability of stock and other company interests, whereas the corporation allows unrestricted transfer. Thus, if your business will require the right to transfer interests without restriction, the LLC is not the right choice. In any event, since laws concerning the LLC vary from state to state, until a uniform LLC law is adopted by all jurisdictions, it is imperative that you thoroughly investigate the LLC regulations for the state in which you intend to do business before deciding on using this form of organization.

CHAPTER 5:
FINANCING YOUR BUSINESS

IN GENERAL

One of the most important aspects of operating a business is maintaining adequate cash flow. One of the leading causes of business failure is insufficient start-up capital. If the business takes off, more money will be needed to carry the increased operational costs, which may include additional inventory and payroll, as well as expansion funds. Basically, you should have enough money to cover the operating expenses of your company for at least one year, including your salary.

Many small business owners use their own money to start their new businesses. Personal savings should be considered the primary source of funds for starting a business. If you haven't started already, start now to begin accumulating cash through personal savings. Overall, small firms rely more on owner capital and less on external debt capital than larger firms.

In addition, small firms are more dependent than large firms on short-term debt relative to long-term debt. Most small firms use external financing only occasionally. Less than half of small firms borrow once or more during a year. However, small firms experiencing rapid growth or those with high volumes of receivables require frequent external financing. Thus, unless personal funds are unlimited, you will have to look to outside financing at some point to keep the business afloat.

Of course, your ability to acquire outside financing depends heavily on whether you are starting the business from scratch or if you are buying an existing business. An existing business will usually have a track record, in which case a lender will be more likely to risk funds, whereas a new business poses a much greater risk. Risking your own funds is an indicator to outside investors of how serious and committed you are about your business.

RAISING CAPITAL

The capital you are seeking to raise will likely be a combination of debt capital and equity capital. Debt capital is the money you raise through loans that are repaid with interest, usually through a bank. Equity capital is the money you raise by giving up some portion of ownership in your business, such as through the sale of stock or a partnership arrangement.

There should be a balance between your debt and equity capital, since too much of either can be bad. If you incur too much debt capital, your company will look unstable, and it is unlikely you will be able to obtain any more financing should the need arise. If you raise too much equity capital, you run the risk of losing control of your business to the investors, who generally require a provision allowing them to replace you if they suspect that you are unable to adequately manage the business. In addition to the assistance provided by the SBA, as discussed below, common sources of debt and equity capital include those described below.

SOURCES OF DEBT CAPITAL

Bank Loans

Access to credit is vital for small business survival, and a key supplier of credit to small firms is the commercial banking system, followed by finance companies, the second most prominent lender to small business. Because banks operate on a relatively low profit margin, they are not in the practice of taking risks. A bank is much more likely to lend money to a successful business which does not need financing to keep the business running, but is seeking funds to expand its operations.

Banks often require a guaranty of payment from the principal shareholders or officers of the company. Thus, if the company defaults in its repayment of credit, the lender can go after the personal assets of the individual guarantors. Most sources of financing or credit rely on the guarantor's numeric credit rating—known as FICO—to determine credit worthiness. FICO is a numeric method, using three digits, to predict the likelihood that a borrower will repay their loan as agreed. FICO scores range from a low of 365 to a high of 850. The score evaluates credit payment history, number of open accounts, overall credit balances and public records such as judgments and liens. Generally, a FICO score above 680 will produce a positive response while a score below this will cause a lender to be cautious. It is advisable to find out what your FICO score is before applying for financing or credit. You can obtain your FICO score through any one of the three major credit-reporting agencies:

EQUIFAX
P.O. Box 740241
Atlanta, GA 30374-0241
Tel: 800-685-1111
Website: http://www.equifax.com

EXPERIAN
P.O. Box 2104
Allen, TX 75013
Tel: 888-EXPERIAN (888-397-3742)
Website: http://www.experian.com

TRANSUNION
P.O. Box 1000
Chester, PA 19022
Tel: 800-916-8800
Website: http://www.transunion.com

The Small Business Administration (SBA) has loan guarantee programs available for start-up businesses. If you are eligible for an SBA guarantee program, your bank will be much more likely to provide financing. The 7(a) Loan Guaranty Program is the SBA's primary loan program, and is discussed more fully below.

The approval of a bank loan—short-term or long-term—generally requires that the business be in good financial standing and that the business offer collateral to secure the loan. There are certain steps you can take in preparing your loan package that may increase your chances of securing financing. You should emphasize your experience and track record in the particular business.

The Business Plan

The first step in successfully obtaining a loan for your small business is to prepare a comprehensive business plan, which should precisely describe your business, including your product or service, key employees of the company, the market, the costs, potential profit, etc. The new business owner will have to demonstrate to the lender or investor the potential of the new business in order to obtain funding. A well-developed business plan is essential in this regard and is a crucial part of any loan package.

The purpose of your business plan is to precisely define your business, its goals, and its potential. It should show your company in the best possible light, without being misleading, and without divulging too much information should a competitor get his or her hands on it. A properly drawn business plan should include as its basic components your company's balance sheets, income statements, and cash flow analyses.

Before you begin formulating your business plan, there are certain steps you should follow:

1. Research your proposed business in detail, including the market, the competition, the sales and profit potential and the amount of start-up money you will need for your particular type of business.

2. Research the location where you will establish your business to make sure it is appropriate for the type of business you are proposing—location can make or break a new business.

3. Gather complete business records, including all financial data that relates to your business.

4. Define your goals and objectives.

A well-organized business plan should include the following components:

Introduction

The introduction should give a detailed description of the business and its goals and discuss the ownership of the business and the legal structure. You should also list the skills and experience you bring to the business and the advantages your business has over its competition.

Marketing

The section on marketing should discuss the product and/or service offered; identify the customer demand for the product and/or service; and identify the market, its size and locations. You should also explain how your product and/or service will be advertised and marketed and explain the pricing strategy.

Financial Management

The section on financial management should explain your source and the amount of initial equity capital. It should set forth a monthly operating budget and an expected return on investment and monthly cash flow for the first year. You should provide projected income statements and balance sheets for a two-year period and discuss your break-even point. You should also explain your personal balance sheet and method of compensation. Discuss who will maintain your accounting records and how they will be kept and address alternative approaches to any problem that may develop.

Operations

The operations section should explain how the business will be managed on a day-to-day basis and discuss hiring and personnel procedures. Insurance, lease or rental agreements, and issues pertinent to your business should be discussed. Explain the equipment necessary to produce the products or services offered by the business, and account for production and delivery of products and services.

Concluding Statement

The concluding statement should summarize your business goals and objectives and express your commitment to the success of your business.

A sample Business Plan Format is set forth at Appendix 15.

Financial Statement

In addition to your business plan, you must generally provide the loan officer with projected cash flow for the first three years of business, a list of collateral available to secure the loan, and a financial statement of your own resources and expenses.

A sample Financial Statement is set forth at Appendix 16.

Repayment of the loan generally is made in installments at various intervals e.g., monthly, quarterly, etc., depending on the duration of the loan. The short-term loan—one maturing in 60 to 90 days—is particularly helpful for the seasonal business.

Banks may also offer what are known as accounts receivable loans, whereby the bank lends on a percentage, e.g. 80%, of the company's outstanding invoices on a short-term basis. The invoice payments are forwarded to the bank, which deducts the loan amount plus interest and forwards the balance to the company. In some cases, the bank will act as a "factor," in which case you actually sell your accounts receivable to the bank, which assumes collection if the customers default in payment.

Line of Credit

A line of credit extended to a company by a bank operates in much the same way as a personal credit card. The lender will generally conduct a credit check before establishing a maximum credit line, which the company can draw upon as needed.

Trade Credit

Delaying payment to suppliers for merchandise received is a form of short-term loan. Suppliers often encourage early payment by discounting invoices that are paid within a certain specified time, e.g., 30 days. On the other hand, payments that are delayed beyond a specified time, e.g., 60 days, will usually incur interest.

Equipment Loans and Leases

When financing is needed to purchase the company's equipment, the equipment itself may serve as collateral for a loan. Alternatively, the company may enter into a leasing agreement whereby the leasing company holds title to the equipment for the duration of the lease, which generally extends for the designated life of the equipment. The company makes payments during the lease period, which in the aggregate will have exceeded the purchase price of the equipment by the end of the lease term. Depending on the lease provisions, at the end of the lease, the company may be able to take title to the equipment for a nominal sum.

The SBA 7(a) Loan Guaranty Program

The 7(a) Loan Guaranty Program is the SBA's primary loan program. The SBA reduces risk to lenders by guaranteeing major portions of loans made to small businesses. This enables the lenders to provide financing to small businesses when funding is otherwise unavailable on reasonable terms. The eligibility requirements and credit criteria of the program are very broad in order to accommodate a wide range of financing needs.

When a small business applies to a lending institution for a loan, the lender reviews the application and decides if it merits a loan on its own or if it requires additional support in the form of an SBA guaranty. The lender then requests SBA backing on the loan. In guaranteeing the loan, the SBA assures the lender that, in the event the borrower does not repay the loan, the government will reimburse the lending institution for a portion of its loss. By providing this guaranty, the SBA is able to help tens of thousands of small businesses every year get financing they would not otherwise obtain.

To qualify for an SBA guaranty, a small business must meet the 7(a) criteria, and the lender must certify that it could not provide funding on reasonable terms except with an SBA guaranty. SBA's 7(a) Loan Program has a maximum loan amount of $2 million. SBA's maximum exposure is $1.5 million. Thus, if a business receives an SBA guaranteed loan for $2 million, the maximum guaranty to the lender will be $1.5 million or 75 percent.

Processing the Loan

The small business owner must submit a loan application to a lender for initial review. If the lender approves the loan subject to an SBA guaranty, a copy of the application and a credit analysis are forwarded by the lender to the nearest SBA office.

A sample Application for Business Loan (SBA Form 4) is set forth at Appendix 17.

After SBA approval, the lending institution closes the loan and disburses the funds. You make monthly loan payments directly to the lender. As with any loan, you are responsible for repaying the full amount of the loan. There are no balloon payments, prepayment penalties, application fees or points permitted with 7(a) loans. Repayment plans may be tailored to each business.

Use of Proceeds

Proceeds from an SBA 7(a) loan may be used to expand or renovate facilities; purchase machinery, equipment, fixtures and leasehold improvements; finance receivables and augment working capital; refinance existing debt with compelling reason; finance seasonal lines of credit; construct commercial buildings; and/or purchase land or buildings.

Loan Term

The length of time for repayment depends on the use of the proceeds and the ability of your business to repay—usually seven years for working capital, and up to 25 years for fixed assets such as the purchase or major renovation of real estate, or for purchase of equipment, but not to exceed the useful life of the equipment.

Interest Rates

Interest rates are negotiated between the borrower and the lender but are subject to SBA maximums, which are pegged to the Prime Rate. Interest rates may be fixed or variable.

Fixed Rate Loans

Fixed rate loans of $50,000 or more must not exceed Prime Plus 2.25 percent if the maturity is less than 7 years, and Prime Plus 2.75 percent if the maturity is 7 years or more.

For loans between $25,000 and $50,000, maximum rates must not exceed Prime Plus 3.25 percent if the maturity is less than 7 years, and Prime Plus 3.75 percent if the maturity is 7 years or more.

For loans of $25,000 or less, the maximum interest rate must not exceed Prime Plus 4.25 percent if the maturity is less than 7 years, and Prime Plus 4.75 percent, if the maturity is 7 years or more.

Variable Rate Loans

Variable rate loans may be pegged to either the lowest prime rate or the SBA optional peg rate. The optional peg rate is a weighted average of rates the federal government pays for loans with maturities similar to the average SBA loan. It is calculated quarterly and published in the "Federal Register."

The lender and the borrower negotiate the amount of the spread which will be added to the base rate. An adjustment period is selected which will identify the frequency at which the note rate will change, however, it must be no more often than monthly, and must be consistent, e.g., monthly, quarterly, etc.

Lender Fees

To offset the cost of the SBA loan programs to the taxpayer, the SBA charges the lender a nominal fee to provide a guaranty. The guaranty fee is based on the maturity of the loan and the dollar amount that the SBA guarantees. The lender may pass this charge on to the applicant after the lender has paid the fee to the SBA, and has made the first loan disbursement. However, the lender's annual service fee to the SBA cannot be passed on to the borrower.

For loans of $150,000 or less, a 2 percent guaranty fee will be charged. Lenders are again permitted to retain 25 percent of the up-front guarantee fee on loans with a gross amount of $150,000 or less.

For loans more than $150,000 but up to and including $700,000, a 3 percent guaranty fee will be charged.

For loans greater than $700,000, a 3.5 percent guaranty fee will be charged.

For loans greater than $1 million, an additional .25 percent guaranty fee will be charged for that portion greater than $1 million. The portion of $1 million or less would be charged a 3.5 percent guaranty fee. The portion greater than $1 million would be charged at 3.75 percent.

The annual on-going servicing fee for all 7(a) loans is 0.545 percent of the outstanding balance of the guaranteed portion of the loan, and this fee remains in effect for the term of the loan.

Collateral

The applicant must pledge sufficient assets, to the extent that they are reasonably available, to adequately secure the loan. Personal guaranties are required from all the principal owners of the business. Liens on personal assets of the principals may be required. However, in most cases a loan will not be declined where insufficient collateral is the only unfavorable factor.

Eligibility

The majority of businesses are eligible for financial assistance from the SBA. However, applicant businesses must: (i) operate for profit; (ii) be engaged in, or propose to do business in, the United States or its possessions; (iii) have reasonable owner equity to invest; and, (iv) use alternative financial resources first including personal assets.

Some businesses are ineligible for financial assistance. For example, businesses cannot be engaged in illegal activities, loan packaging, speculation, multi sales distribution, gambling, investment or lending, or where the owner is on parole.

A small business must also fall within the size standards set by the SBA in order to be eligible for a 7(a) loan. The SBA determines if the business qualifies as a small business based on the average number of employees during the preceding 12 months or on sales averaged over the previous three years.

The maximum size standards of the business are as follows:

1. Agriculture – Average annual revenues ranging from $750,000 to $11.5 million

2. Animal Production – Average annual revenues ranging from $0.75 million to $11.5 million

3. Forestry/Logging – 500 employees/Average annual revenues ranging from $4 million to $16.5 million

4. Fishing/Hunting/Trapping – Average annual revenue of $4 million

5. Mining – 500 employees/Average annual revenues of $6.5 million

6. Utilities – 500 employees/Average annual revenues ranging from $6.5 million to $11.5 million

7. Construction – Average annual revenues ranging from $6.5 million to $31 million

8. Manufacturing – Ranges from 500 to 1,500 employees depending on the product being manufactured

9. Wholesale Trade – 100 employees

10. Retail Trade – Average annual revenues ranging from $6.5 million to $26.5 million

11. Transportation – Ranges from 500 to 1,500 employees, depending on type of transportation business/Average annual revenues ranging from $6.5 million to $31.5 million

12. Information Services – Ranges from 500 to 1,500 employees, depending on type of information service/Average annual revenues ranging from $6.5 million to $27 million

13. Finance/Insurance – 1,500 employees/Annual revenues ranging from $65 million to $165 million

14. Real Estate/Rental/Leasing – Average annual revenues ranging from $2 million to $23.5 million

15. Professional/Scientific/Technical – Ranges from 150 to 1,500 employees, depending on type of business/Average annual revenues ranging from $6.5 million to $25 million

16. Management – Average annual revenues of $6.5 million

17. Administrative and Support – 500 employees/Average annual revenues ranging from $6.5 million to $32.5 million

18. Educational Services – Average annual revenues ranging from $6.5 million to $32.5 million

19. Health Care and Social Assistance – Average annual revenues ranging from $6.5 million to $31.5 million

20. Arts/Entertainment/Recreation – Average annual revenues of $6.5 million dollars

21. Accommodation and Food Services – Average annual revenues ranging from $6.5 million to $19 million

22. Other Services – Average annual revenues ranging from $6.5 million to $23 million

SOURCES OF EQUITY CAPITAL

Small Business Investment Companies

Under the Small Business Investment Act, the SBA licenses privately owned small business investment companies (SBICs) which provide funds to eligible small businesses. The SBIC generally raises its investment funds by borrowing from the federal government or banks.

Like the SBA, the SBIC also requires that the small business be unable to raise money through other channels. Although SBICs are more willing to take risks on new businesses, they are profit-motivated organizations and, thus, will closely examine the profit potential of your business.

Venture Capital Companies

Another source of funding for small businesses—usually on a short-term basis—is a venture capital company. Venture capital companies are in the business of taking risks in return for larger returns and, thus they will generally want to take an active role in your business. You may obtain information on venture capital from the SBA, as well as from your investment adviser, banker, lawyer and accountant.

Individual Investors

You may be able to raise money by bringing in investors with whom you will share the profits, if any, from your business. Such investors can be known individuals, such as relatives, friends and business associates, and may also include unknown investors, such as ex-entrepreneurs and wealthy business people, who have money to invest. Like venture capital companies, private investors often desire to take an active control in the business.

SBA DISASTER RELIEF LOAN PROGRAM

If your property is damaged as a result of a disaster, you can apply to the SBA for a disaster relief loan. The amount of money that the SBA will lend is based upon the actual cost of repairing or replacing the property, minus any insurance settlements or other reimbursements or grants, up to a set limit.

When applying for a disaster relief loan, you need to include certain information and documentation. The required information is specified in the SBA loan application. In all cases, it includes an itemized list of losses with the repair or replacement cost of each item. It also includes permission for the IRS to give the SBA information from your last two federal income tax returns. If you have pictures of the damaged property, you can include them as well.

The SBA Disaster Business Loan Application is set forth at Appendix 18.

Once you have returned your loan application, an SBA loss verifier will visit you to determine the extent of the damage and the reasonableness of the loan request. The SBA attempts to make a decision on the application within 7 to 21 days, however, the SBA disaster relief program is not an immediate emergency relief program. It is a loan program to help you in your long-term rebuilding and repairing. Therefore, the SBA must carefully review the loan application and documentation to make sure you can repay the loan.

Loans over $10,000 have to be secured by collateral. Usually, the security consists of a first or second mortgage on the damaged real estate.

After the loan is approved, the SBA will tell you what additional documentation is needed to close the loan. Once all of the loan closing documents is returned to the SBA, the SBA will fund the loan in installments for specific and designated purposes to repair or replace the damage. The funds cannot be used for any other purpose than to return the property to its previous condition. The penalty for misusing disaster funds is the immediate repayment of one-and-a-half times the original amount of the loan. The SBA requires that you obtain receipts and maintain good records of all loan expenditures as you restore your damaged property and that you keep these receipts and records for three years.

SBA 8(a) BD Program for Small Disadvantaged Businesses

The Small Business Administration has created a business development program to help small disadvantaged businesses compete in the American economy and gain access to the federal procurement market. The program is known as an 8(a) BD Program, named for the section of the Small Business Act that instituted the program.

Basic Eligibility Requirements

In order to be eligible for the 8(a) BD program, a company must be a small business, that is unconditionally owned and controlled by one or more socially and economically disadvantaged individuals who are of good character and citizens of the United States. The company must also be able to demonstrate a potential for success.

Small Business Determination

The SBA defines a small business as one that is independently owned and operated, organized for profit, and not dominant in its field. Depending on the industry, size standard eligibility is based on the average number of employees, or average annual revenue, set forth in Chapter 2 of this almanac.

Socially Disadvantaged Individuals

For purposes of the program, socially disadvantaged individuals are defined as those individuals who have been subjected to racial or ethnic prejudice or cultural bias because of their identity as members of a group. Social disadvantage must stem from circumstances beyond their control. In the absence of evidence to the contrary, individuals who are members of the following designated groups are presumed to be socially disadvantaged:

1. Black Americans;

2. Hispanic Americans;

3. Native Americans, including American Indians, Eskimos, Aleuts, and Native Hawaiians;

4. Asian Pacific Americans, including persons with origins from Japan, China, the Philippines, Vietnam, Korea, Samoa, Guam, U.S. Trust Territory of the Pacific Islands, the Republic of Palau, the Commonwealth of the Northern Mariana Islands, Laos, Cambodia, Kampuchea, Taiwan, Burma, Thailand, Malaysia, Indonesia, Singapore, Brunei, Republic of the Marshall Islands, Federated States of Micronesia, Macao, Hong Kong, Fiji, Tonga, Kiribati, Tuvalu, or Nauru;

5. Subcontinent Asian Americans, including persons with origins from India, Pakistan, Bangladesh, Sri Lanka, Bhutan, the Maldives Islands or Nepal; and

6. Members of other groups designated by the SBA as socially disadvantaged individuals.

Nonmembers of a Designated Group

An individual who is not a member of a designated group must establish social disadvantage on the basis of a "preponderance of evidence." Generally, preponderance is evidence of quality and quantity which leads the decision maker to conclude, objectively, that it is more probable than not that the individual is socially disadvantaged.

An individual seeking socially disadvantaged status must establish:

1. at least one objective distinguishing feature that has contributed to social disadvantage, e.g., race, ethnic origin, gender, physical handicap, long-term residence in an environment isolated from the mainstream of American society, or another similar cause not common to individuals who are not socially disadvantaged;

2. personal experiences of substantial and chronic social disadvantage, occurring in American society, stemming from the foregoing objective distinguishing feature; and

3. negative impact on the individual's entry into or advancement in the business world because of the disadvantage. In every case, however, the SBA considers education, employment and business history, where applicable, to see if the totality of circumstances shows disadvantage in entering or advancing in the business world.

Evidence may include:

1. Court or administrative findings of discrimination.

2. Statements made under oath to an investigator or in a court or administrative proceeding.

3. Affidavits or statements sworn under oath by an individual owner that have specific recurrent incidents of discrimination or a pattern of discrimination over a significant period of time. Nevertheless, applicant statements alone, without supporting or corroborating evidence will be given less weight than if corroborated.

4. Sworn affidavits or statements from third parties that corroborate or support the assertions made by the owner. Affidavits from independent third parties who do not have an interest in or close relationship to the owner will have more weight than statements by relatives or friends of the owner.

5. Documentary evidence that corroborates or supports assertions made by an owner regarding specific incidents or a pattern of discrimination. Such documentation includes:

(a) personnel records;

(b) payroll records;

(c) rejection letters on job applications;

(d) denials of credit application;

(e) documents relating to rejected contract offers, i.e., bid abstracts, solicitations, etc.;

(f) contemporaneous records memorializing meetings, conversations, negotiations, telephone calls, etc.

(g) documents setting forth company policies which are alleged to be discriminatory.

In addition, evidence which tends to show generalized patterns of discrimination against a non-designated group, or statistical data showing that businesses owned by a specific non-designated group are disproportionately underrepresented in a particular industry, may be used to augment an individual's case.

Although statistics and generalized patterns are not sufficient by themselves to establish a case of individual social disadvantage, an individual's statement of personal experiences in combination with the generalized evidence may be sufficient to demonstrate social disadvantage.

Economically Disadvantaged Individual

For purposes of the program, socially disadvantaged individuals are defined as those individuals whose ability to compete in the free enterprise system has been impaired due to diminished capital and credit opportunities. In evaluating whether an individual is economically disadvantaged, the SBA takes into the account the following factors:

1. The individual's net worth, after excluding the individual's equity in the company and equity in the primary residence. The individual's net worth may not exceed $250,000.

2. The individual's average two-year income.

3. The fair market value of all of the individual's assets.

4. The individual's access to credit and capital.

5. The financial condition of the applicant's company.

In addition to the above, the SBA will include any assets that the individual transferred to an immediate family member for less than market value within two year's prior to the company's application for participation in the program. A transfer of assets for fair market value would be excluded provided the applicant supplies verifiable independent documentation of the value of the assets.

Also excluded from the individual's net worth are transfers for education, medical expenses, certain forms of essential support, and transfers that are consistent with the customary recognition of special occasions—e.g. birthdays, graduations, anniversaries, and retirements. The disadvantaged applicant must show proof of the reasons for these asset transfers.

Ownership and Control

As set forth above, in order to be eligible for the 8(a) BD program, a company must be unconditionally owned and controlled by one or more socially and economically disadvantaged individuals. The SBA requires at least 51% ownership by the disadvantaged individuals. Control is not the same as ownership. Control includes both strategic policy setting and the day-to-day management and administration of business operations by the disadvantaged individuals.

The SBA does not require that the disadvantaged individual have the technical or licensing expertise, but does require them to have management experience to the extent necessary to run the company. Nevertheless, the disadvantaged individual must demonstrate that he or she has ultimate managerial and supervisory control over those in the company who have the technical or licensing expertise.

Role of Non-Disadvantaged Individuals

Non-disadvantaged individuals may be involved in the ownership and management of an applicant company, however, a non-disadvantaged individual or immediate family member may not:

1. exercise actual control or have the power to control the applicant company;

2. be a former employer or principal of a former employer of any disadvantaged owner of the applicant company; or

3. receive compensation from the applicant company in any form that exceeds the compensation to be received by the highest officer. The highest-ranking officer may elect to take a lower salary than a non-disadvantaged individual only upon demonstrating that it helps the applicant company.

If one or more of the above situations exist, the non-disadvantaged individual will be found to control the company.

Evaluating Potential Success

For purposes of the program, in determining the company's potential for success, the SBA considers the following factors:

1. the technical and managerial experience of the applicant company's managers;

2. the company's operating history;

3. the ability of the company to access credit and capital;

4. the company's financial capacity;

5. the company's record of performance; and

6. whether the applicant company, or individuals employed by the company, holds the requisite licenses if the company is engaged in an industry requiring professional licensing.

In addition, the applicant company must have been operating for at least two full years as evidenced by business income tax returns, and the operating revenues must be generated in the same industry in which the applicant company is seeking 8(a) BD program certification. If the company has not been in business for two full years, it must obtain a waiver of this requirement by meeting the following conditions:

1. The individual or individuals upon whom eligibility is based must have substantial business management experience.

2. The applicant company must demonstrate the technical experience to carry out its business plan with a substantial likelihood for success.

3. The applicant company must have adequate capital to sustain its operations and carry out its business plan.

4. The applicant company must have a record of successful performance on contracts from governmental or non-governmental sources in its primary industry category.

5. The applicant company must have, or must be able to demonstrate that it has, the ability to timely obtain the personnel, facilities, equipment, and any other requirements needed to perform on contracts if it is admitted to the 8(a) BD program.

Good Character Requirement

As set forth above, in order to be eligible for the 8(a) BD program, the disadvantaged individual who owns and controls the applicant company must be of "good character." The SBA may determine that the disadvantaged individual lacks good character based on the following circumstances:

1. adverse information regarding possible criminal conduct by the applicant and its principals;

2. violations of SBA regulations;

3. debarment or suspension of the company and/or individual;

4. lack of business integrity as demonstrated by information related to an indictment or guilty plea, conviction, civil judgment, or settlement;

5. principals of the company are currently incarcerated, or on parole or probation; or

6. evidence that the company knowingly submitted false information during the application process.

Application Process

The SBA provides prospective applicants with additional information on eligibility and the application process, as well as the forms required to apply for the 8(a) BD program. The SBA also holds orientation workshops at certain SBA district offices. The SBA has designed the application forms so that the applicant can complete the forms without hiring professional help.

The regional Division of Program Certification and Eligibility (DPCE) has 15 days to review the application for completeness. If the application is incomplete, the applicant will have 15 days to provide additional information. If the DPCE determines the application is complete, a final decision regarding 8(a) BD Program eligibility will be made within 90 days after the SBA's determination that the application is complete.

If the application is declined, the applicant has the right to request that the SBA reconsider the declined application by filing a written request for reconsideration within 45 days after receiving notice that the application was declined. The applicant has the burden of overcoming each reason cited in the SBA's decision to decline the application. During the reconsideration process, the applicant must provide any additional information and documentation necessary to overcome the reasons for the initial decline.

If an application is declined after reconsideration, the SBA will not accept a new application until twelve (12) months after the date of the final decision on reconsideration. In addition, if an applicant is declined solely on issues of social disadvantage, economic disadvantage, ownership, control, or any combination of these four criteria, the declined applicant may appeal the decision to the SBA's Office of Hearings and Appeals (OHA).

The applicant can file the appeal to the OHA after receiving the initial decision to decline the application, or after receiving a negative decision after reconsideration. The OHA will examine the decision to determine whether it was arbitrary, capricious, or contrary to law, however, no new or revised information is considered during the appeal process.

Annual Review

Companies in the 8(a) BD program are reviewed annually by the SBA for compliance with the eligibility requirements. As part of the annual review, each company must submit the following:

1. a certification that it meets the 8(a) BD program eligibility requirements;

2. a certification that there have been no changed circumstances which could adversely affect the company's program eligibility;

3. personal financial information for each disadvantaged owner;

4. a record from each individual claiming disadvantaged status regarding the transfer of assets for less than fair market value to any immediate family member, or to a trust in which an immediate family member is a beneficiary, within two years of the date of the annual review. The record must provide the name of the recipient and family relationship and the difference between the fair market value of the

asset transferred and the value received by the disadvantaged individual;

5. a record of all payments, compensation, and distributions, including loans, advances, salaries, and dividends, made by the company to each of its owners, officers, directors, or to any person or entity affiliated with such individuals;

6. request for Copy or Transcript of Tax Form (IRS Form 4506); and

7. such other information that the SBA may deem necessary.

If the company fails to provide the required documentation for the annual review, the SBA may initiate termination proceedings against the company.

Termination

Termination refers to the exit of an 8(a) BD certified company from the program before the expiration of the program term for good cause. Examples of good cause include, but are not limited to the following:

1. Submission of false information in the company's 8(a) BD application, regardless of whether correct information would have caused the company to be denied admission to the program, and regardless of whether correct information was given to the SBA in accompanying documents or by other means.

2. Failure by the company to maintain its eligibility for program participation.

3. Failure by the company for any reason, including the death of an individual upon whom eligibility was based, to maintain ownership, full-time day-to-day management, and control by disadvantaged individuals.

4. Failure by the company to obtain prior written approval from the SBA for any changes in ownership or business structure, management, or control.

5. Failure by the company to disclose to the SBA the extent to which non-disadvantaged persons or firms participate in the management of the company.

6. Failure by the company, or one or more of the company's principals, to maintain good character.

7. A pattern of failure to make required submissions or responses to the SBA in a timely manner, including a failure to provide required financial statements, requested tax returns, reports, updated business plans, information requested by the SBA's Office of Inspector

General, or other requested information or data within 30 days of the date of request.

8. Cessation of business operations by the company.

9. Failure by the company to pursue competitive and commercial business in accordance with its business plan, or failure in other ways to make reasonable efforts to develop and achieve competitive viability.

10. A pattern of inadequate performance by the company of awarded section 8(a) BD contracts.

11. Failure by the company to pay or repay significant financial obligations owed to the Federal Government.

12. Failure by the company to obtain and keep current any and all required permits, licenses, and charters, including suspension or revocation of any professional license required to operate the business.

13. Excessive withdrawals, including transfers of funds or other business assets, from the company for the personal benefit of any of its owners or any person or entity affiliated with the owners that hinder the development of the company.

14. Unauthorized use of SBA direct or guaranteed loan proceeds or violation of an SBA loan agreement.

15. Conduct by the company, or any of its principals, indicating a lack of business integrity. Such conduct may be demonstrated by information related to a criminal indictment or guilty plea, a criminal conviction, or a judgment or settlement in a civil case.

16. Willful failure by the company to comply with applicable labor standards and obligations.

17. Material breach of any terms and conditions of the 8(a) BD Program Participation Agreement.

18. Willful violation by a company, or any of its principals, of any SBA regulation pertaining to material issues.

Length of Participation in 8(a) BD Program

Participation in the 8(a) BD program is divided into two stages:

1. The Developmental Stage—The developmental stage is four years and is designed to help 8(a) BD certified companies overcome their economic disadvantage by providing business development assistance.

2. The Transitional Stage—The transitional stage is five years and is designed to help participants overcome the remaining elements of

economic disadvantage and prepare participants for leaving the 8(a) BD program.

A company "graduates" from the 8(a) BD program at the expiration of the term of the program.

CHAPTER 6:
EMPLOYER/EMPLOYEE RELATIONS

RECRUITING JOB APPLICANTS

If you don't have the time to devote to interviewing and checking the background of prospective employees, there are companies that specialize in screening suitable job applicants.

State Employment Services

Every state has some sort of government employment service affiliated with the U.S. Employment Services, that assists businesses in recruiting employees. The employment service will screen the prospective employee and administer aptitude tests to determine if he or she possesses the skills necessary to fill the position you specify.

Employment Agencies

Employment agencies find suitable permanent employees for businesses in return for a fee. The agency undertakes the screening process, including administering aptitude tests and performing background checks on prospective employees.

If you only need extra help during your busy times, e.g., for taking inventory or for holiday sales, a temporary employment agency provides the services of temporary employees. The service is responsible for paying the temporary worker, and all other employee-related benefits and costs.

Online Classifieds

Most major newspapers have their help wanted ads posted on the Internet. In addition, there are job search sites that assist in matching employers and employees.

College Interns

Most colleges have intern programs in which a student works part-time or volunteers as an intern in return for college credit. The student's goal is to gain some actual experience in the field they are studying. For example, a communications major would seek an internship at a radio station, and an accounting student would look for an internship in a corporate setting. You can contact a local college to find out more about their internship program.

Help Wanted Ads

You can try and recruit prospective employees by advertising in the classified section of your local newspaper. Make sure your ad spells out the skills a prospective employee should have, including education and experience, if required for the position.

HIRING EMPLOYEES

Managing an efficient, competent staff of employees is crucial to the success of your business. Thus, the hiring of employees should be carried out very carefully. You must look at your business from beginning to end, and consider what tasks must be carried out to accomplish its purpose. Largely depending upon the nature of your business, you must determine the number of employees you need and the responsibilities you want those employees to undertake.

Determining the number of employees you need to operate your business efficiently can be difficult and often cannot be predicted until you have been in business for a period of time. Of course, depending on the type of business you operate, it may be easier to determine the number of employees needed in certain departments. For example, if you operate a clothing manufacturing business, and you have ten sewing machines, you will need ten employees to operate those machines. You may want to have one or two back-up employees who perform other tasks, but who can also operate the machine when the regular operator is out sick or on vacation.

Determining the number of employees you need also depends on the efficiency of a particular employee. Some employees have the ability to do the work of two or three standard employees. On the other hand, two less able employees may only be able to accomplish as much as one standard employee. If you find an employee who turns out to be particularly valuable to the company, you may wish to enter into an employment agreement with him or her.

A sample employment agreement is set forth at Appendix 19.

Before you begin hiring, refer to the organizational chart included in your business plan to determine what tasks each department of your company will undertake. You can then determine the smallest number of employees you believe you need to accomplish all of those tasks, and prepare a realistic job description for each employee in each department. You should also prepare a qualifications sheet listing the requirements of each particular position, such as level of education and experience. This will at least give you a starting point. It is far easier, and more economical, to hire additional employees as needed than to fire existing employees, and risk exposure to legal claims, however unsubstantiated their claims may be.

For example, if you are hiring an employee that will be dealing with the public, such as a salesperson, you should make sure he or she possesses good customer service skills. He or she should be articulate, courteous, helpful and have a neat, presentable appearance. In addition, the employee must be knowledgeable about the products your business offers.

Employee Handbook

You should consider preparing an employee handbook detailing the written policies and procedures of the company which each employee is expected to follow. Items covered in the employee handbook may include company dress code, vacation, holiday and sick leave policies, employee benefits, company hours, company policy concerning performance evaluations and salary increases, and disciplinary procedures. This handbook is quite important, as it puts the employee on notice as to what behaviors are expected and what behaviors will not be tolerated.

Employee Polygraph Protection Act

When interviewing a prospective employee, one trait an employer looks for is honesty. Of course, this trait is not often readily apparent during a 15-minute job interview. Employers might wish to conduct a lie detector test of every employee. However, under the Employee Polygraph Protection Act, most private employers are prohibited from using lie detector tests either for hiring employees or for existing employees.

There are certain exemptions to the Act. For example, the federal, state, and local governments are not subject to the law. In addition, private employers who are engaged in the manufacture, distribution, or dispensing of pharmaceuticals, and security services, such as security guard services, are permitted to administer lie detector tests to certain prospective employees, subject to restrictions. There are also situations in which the Act permits testing of persons suspected of employee theft that resulted in economic loss to the employer, also subject to restrictions.

In those situations where lie detector tests are legally permitted, the employee has certain rights relating to the length and conduct of the test. In addition, the employer is required to give the employee advance written notice. An employee may refuse to take the test or may request to discontinue taking the test during its administration. The results of an employee's lie detector test are private and are not permitted to be disclosed to any unauthorized person.

Violations of the Act may result in civil penalties up to $10,000. Such a legal action may be brought by a job applicant, an employee, or by the Secretary of Labor. In addition, where a specific state law or collective bargaining agreement provides for a more restrictive ban on lie detector tests, the federal government defers to that law.

Drug and Alcohol Testing

It is a fact that drug and alcohol abuse by employees costs employers billions of dollars in medical costs, liability insurance and decreased productivity. Employees who use drugs and/or alcohol have a high rate of absenteeism. For this reason, more and more employees have instituted drug and alcohol testing for all job applicants as well as current employees.

In general, state and federal laws have been passed to allow employers to test their employees for on-the-job drug or alcohol abuse. Employers are taking advantage of these laws and, in some cases, have made drug and alcohol testing mandatory.

For example, Congress enacted the Omnibus Transportation Employee Testing Act of 1991, which requires mass transit operators who receive federal funds to conduct pre-employment, reasonable suspicion, random and post-accident testing for those employees responsible for safety-sensitive functions. Employees who fail the test are subject to immediate removal from their positions. Mass transit operators who do not comply with the mandatory drug testing law risk losing their federal funding.

The United States Supreme Court has upheld federal mandatory drug testing laws with the requirement that the employee being subject to testing be employed in a safety-sensitive position. The basis for upholding such testing is that it serves an important governmental interest. Thus, if an employee works in a safety-sensitive position within the federal government, they are subject to drug and alcohol testing.

Following in the footsteps of the federal government, states have also enacted laws subjecting employees to drug and alcohol testing. Presently, 32 states have enacted employment drug or alcohol testing laws.

HANDLING EMPLOYEE THEFT

Employee theft can have a serious detrimental effect on a business. Employee theft can range from stealing petty cash to hiring fictitious personnel and collecting their salaries. Your first defense against employee theft is in the hiring process. You should carefully screen every potential employee, making sure to check the applicant's references. Ideally, a professional background check may save you money in the long run by ruling out a prospective employee who is revealed to be a convicted burglar. The greater the access to company money or other valuables, the more extensive your investigation should be.

An efficient security system should be installed on the premises, as well as a computer security program to detect employee fraud or record tampering. You can also set up a system of checks and balances whereby no one employee has sufficient control over a particular task that they are able to complete the theft. For example, one employee may check invoices for accuracy, and another employee may be responsible for issuing the checks. Nevertheless, you should also be aware of the possibility of collusion among two or more employees.

Employee theft may be discovered in a variety of ways, such as by departmental audits or direct observation. Often, co-workers of the offending employee are aware of the problem, but do not know how to confront the issue. Information on the ethical obligations for the discovery and reporting of suspected employee theft may be included in the employee handbook and made available to all employees, as well as management personnel. The materials may include guidelines that assist the individual in proper and discreet reporting procedures.

If, despite your best efforts, employee theft is suspected, it would be wise to conduct a thorough investigation without making hasty accusations. All relevant documentation should be obtained and carefully reviewed. Conduct confidential interviews with employees who may be able to shed some light on the situation. Take care not to alienate your employees, but encourage them to assist you in resolving the situation. Following the interview, request that the employee interviewed sign a statement outlining the conversation. Give the employee the opportunity to correct the statement, based on his or her recollection of the events.

If your investigation uncovers and identifies employee theft, set up a confidential meeting with the offending employee. A memo outlining the allegations and proposed disciplinary action should be given to the employee, with a space provided for the employee to review the charges and respond in writing. If the employee is terminated, a follow-up letter summarizing the exit interview should be mailed to the employee. It is important to maintain as much documentation as possible concerning the termination of employment in case the company should be sued by the employee at a later date.

THE IMMIGRATION REFORM AND CONTROL ACT

The federal Immigration Reform and Control Act of 1990 (IRCA) is a mechanism by which illegal immigration is controlled through the employment system. The IRCA, which is governed by the U.S. Citizenship and Immigration Service (USCIS), requires public and private employers to determine that each person hired is legally authorized to work. The IRCA is comprised of two parts—the anti-discrimination provision and the employer sanction provision.

The anti-discrimination provision prohibits employment discrimination based on national origin and citizenship status and requires that employers treat all job applicants equally. Employers who violate this provision, or retaliate against employees who file discrimination charges, are subject to monetary sanctions ranging up to $2,000 per individual for the first offense, up to $5,000 per individual for the second offense, and up to $10,000 per individual for subsequent offenses.

The employer sanction provision is concerned with the hiring of undocumented workers. Under this provision, employers must complete Form I-9, which is used to verify the employment eligibility and identity of employees. The I-9 form must be completed and retained by the employer for any employees hired after November 6, 1986. The employer must file the I-9 form within three days from the hiring date.

A sample Employment Eligibility Verification Form (DHS Form I-9) is set forth at Appendix 20.

In order to complete the form, the employer must review documentation provided by the employee which satisfies the employment eligibility and identity requirement. The employer cannot request a particular form of identification. Rather, the employee is free to choose from any of the forms of identification acceptable to the U.S. Citizen and Immigration Services (USCIS), an agency organized under the Department of Homeland Security. The USCIS took the place of the Immigration and Naturalization Service (INS).

A list of forms of identification that can be used to satisfy the requirements of the IRCA is set forth at Appendix 21.

Individuals who were employed prior to November 6, 1986 are not subject to the IRCA, and the employer cannot be penalized for retaining those employees, even if they are illegal aliens. However, if any documents provided to the employer are time-dated, employment eligibility should be re-verified.

The IRCA imposes the same monetary sanctions against employers who violate the employer sanction provision as those who violate the anti-discrimination provision. In addition, an employer who does not file the I-9 form is also subject to penalties ranging up to $1,000 per employee.

SETTING EMPLOYEE SALARIES

Some factors which should be considered in establishing appropriate salaries include the level of skill required for the particular position, the importance of the position to the company, the geographic location of your business, and the rate of pay for similar positions with other companies.

Of course, the more valuable an employee is to the company, the higher salary that employee deserves. There is no such thing as a governmentally set maximum wage; thus, this figure may be agreed upon entirely between you and your prospective employee. However, as explained more fully below, there are federally mandated minimum wage laws.

Minimum Wage Laws

Under the Fair Labor Standards Act, an employee has certain rights concerning wages. For example, there is a federal minimum wage requirement that supersedes any state minimum wage laws that would otherwise allow employers to pay employees less than the federal minimum. However, federal minimum wage laws defer to the state's minimum wage law where the state sets a higher minimum wage than the federal government.

A Table of State Minimum Wage Laws is set forth at Appendix 22.

Nevertheless, the Department of Labor may issue special certificates that allow the employer to pay less than the minimum wage to certain employees, which may include certain disabled workers and apprentices.

Overtime Pay

Overtime pay must be at least one and one-half times the employee's regular rate of pay for all hours worked over 40 in a workweek. Some employers will give their employees extra time off from work instead of paying overtime wages. This is known as compensatory time because it ompensates the employee for the extra hours worked.

However, unless the employer is a state or government agency, the substitution of compensatory time for premium pay is generally unlawful. In those situations where compensatory time is legal, the employer must grant the employee leave time that is one and one-half times the hours worked.

For example, if an employee works 50 hours in a regular 40 hour week, he or she is entitled to 15 hours of compensatory time, i.e., the 10 additional hours worked multiplied by one and one-half.

Compensatory time is also subject to a mutual agreement between the employer and employee, or pursuant to an agreement made by union representatives on behalf of the employees. Additional rules may apply when compensatory time is permitted in the private sector; therefore, the reader is advised to check the law of his or her jurisdiction.

Penalties

There are stiff civil and criminal penalties available for employers who do not abide by the law. Employers may be assessed up to $1,000 per violation if they willfully or repeatedly violate the minimum wage or overtime pay provisions of the law. In addition, the Department of Labor may recover back wages for employees who have been underpaid in violation of the law, and those employers found to be in violation may face civil or criminal action against them.

The reader may obtain additional information concerning state minimum wage laws and wage and hour provisions by contacting their state department of labor.

A Directory of State Departments of Labor is set forth at Appendix 23.

CHILD LABOR

The government regulates the use of child labor. In general, an employee must be at least 16 years of age to work in most non-farm jobs, and at least 18 to work in non-farm occupations that are declared hazardous by the Secretary of Labor. Children who are 14 or 15 years old may work during non-school hours in certain specified positions, provided they work no more than three hours on a school day or 18 hours in a school week, and no more than eight hours on a non-school day or 40 hours in a non-school week. There are also certain restrictions on the times of day that a child is permitted to work. Violations of the child labor provisions of the law can result in fines of up to $10,000 per child.

For more information o̶...
it applies to your busi̶

U.S. Department ̶
Employment Sta̶
Wage and Hour̶
Washington, D.̶

INDEPENDENT CONTRA̶

During the course of you̶
perform certain tasks as an̶
contractor is generally defined as̶ a̶
to perform services for that person, but wn̶o̶ ̶
other nor subject to the other's right to control with respect to services
performed.

A sample Independent Contractor Agreement Is set forth at Appendix 24.

An independent contractor is not an employee. Therefore, the business owner does not have to withhold tax from the independent contractor's checks, nor does the employer have to contribute to Social Security or unemployment tax on behalf of the independent contractor.

At times, the IRS may attempt to reclassify an independent contractor as an employee. This can be very costly to the employer because the employer would then be liable for withholding tax, Social Security contributions, and unemployment tax withholding, as well as penalties and interest on those amounts due.

To determine whether or not an individual is likely to be reclassified by the IRS from independent contractor status to employee status, courts have established 20 common law factors which must be taken into account. The factors that may indicate employee status are the following:

1. The worker is required to comply with the employer's instruction as to when, where, and how he is to work.

2. The employer trains the worker to perform in a particular manner.

3. The employer requires the worker to render personal service.

4. The employer hires, supervises, and pays the worker's staff.

5. The employer and the worker have a continuing relationship.

6. The worker is required to work during hours set by the employer.

7. The worker is required to work full-time for the employer.

8. The worker performs the work on the employer's premises, particularly if the work could be performed elsewhere.

...m services in a particu-

...written reports to the

...h as opposed to a per

...r traveling expenses.

...materials to the worker.

...y the worker in the facilities re-

...d (ii) dependence on the employer for

...r facilities.

15. The worker realizes no profit or loss as a result of the services rendered.

16. The worker works exclusively for the employer.

17. The worker does not make his or her services available to the general public.

18. The employer maintains the right to discharge the worker, which would not be possible if the individual were an independent contractor working under a contract.

19. The worker has the right to end the relationship with the employer without continuing to render services. An independent contractor would be bound by the contract to finish the job.

20. The worker's services are integral to the business operations.

In addition to the above criteria, Section 530 of the Revenue Act of 1978 serves as a safe harbor for employers who treated individuals as independent contractors for federal employment tax purposes, even if they were in error, as long as the employer had a reasonable basis for doing so.

A list of IRS factors classifying independent contractors is set forth at Appendix 25.

PAYROLL DEDUCTIONS

As set forth below, employers are required to withhold taxes and other deductions from their employees' salaries, make periodic deposits, and file quarterly payroll tax returns.

Federal Income Tax

Federal income tax is money withheld from an employee's earnings based on gross income, number of dependents, marital status, etc.

Federal Unemployment Tax

Federal unemployment taxes are employer-paid taxes.

State Income Tax

Approximately 41 states require the employer to withhold state income tax.

State Unemployment Insurance Tax

State Unemployment Insurance Tax is determined and controlled by the employer and is determined by the company's own unemployment experience.

State Disability Insurance

State Disability Insurance is assessed on employees by some states, and is determined by setting a maximum withholding amount and/or a wage base.

Social Security

Social Security is paid by both the employer and employee. The employer is responsible for collection and payment of the employee's contribution.

Medicare

Medicare is collected on the basis of a percentage of the first $135,000 of income.

EMPLOYEE HEALTH AND SAFETY

In General

A number of laws now establish basic safety standards which have as their goal a reduction in the number of workplace deaths, injuries and illnesses. All businesses are now required by law to provide a safe and healthy workplace for their employees. Small business owners can engage the services of the growing number of workplace safety consultants, who specialize in bringing companies into compliance with the law.

Some safety precautions the small business owner can take include regular in-house safety inspections, a comprehensive safety plan for all employees, and the maintenance of adequate protective clothing and equipment where the nature of business operations requires such precautions. There should also be an adequately stocked first-aid kit readily available, and the telephone numbers for emergency medical assistance should be on display for quick reference if the need arises.

The Occupational Safety and Health Act

The Occupational Safety and Health Act of 1970, provides job safety and health protection for workers by promoting safe and healthful working conditions throughout the nation. The Act is administered by the Occupational Safety and Health Administration (OSHA), a division of the U.S. Department of Labor. OSHA is responsible for issuing standards relating to the occupational safety and health standards.

Under the Act, employers are required to maintain their facilities free from any recognized hazards that are causing, or are likely to cause, death or serious harm to an employee. On the other hand, employees are also required to comply with all applicable sections of the occupational safety and health standards issued by OSHA.

If an employer is determined to be in violation of the law after an inspection is conducted by an OSHA representative, OSHA may issue a citation against that employer. The citation specifies each and every violation alleged to have been committed by the employer and the date by which the violation must be corrected. The employer is required to display the citation at or near the location of the alleged violation for a period of three days or until the violation is corrected, whichever date is later. The purpose of this provision is to warn the employees about the dangerous condition.

The penalties for failure to adhere to the Act are serious. For example, there are mandatory civil penalties of up to $7,000 per violation against employers for serious violations of the law, and optional penalties of up to $7,000 for nonserious violations. If an employer fails to correct a violation within the allotted time period, additional penalties of up to $7,000 per day can be assessed until the violation is finally corrected.

Willful violations of the Act can result in penalties ranging from a minimum of $5,000 to a maximum of $70,000. Repeated violations can also result in a fine of up to $70,000, and an employer can be assessed a penalty of up to $7,000 for failure to display the citation as required.

In addition to the civil penalties, criminal penalties may be assessed if a willful violation of the Act results in the death of an employee. Upon conviction, such a violation is punishable by a fine of up to $250,000 or by imprisonment of up to six months, or both. If the employer is a corporation, the maximum fine is $500,000. There are additional penalties that may be imposed for subsequent convictions.

OSHA offers free assistance in identifying and correcting workplace safety and health hazards to employers. Employers requesting such assistance are not subject to citation or penalty. OSHA has a 24-hour hotline available for reporting workplace safety and health emergencies (1-800-321-OSHA).

A Directory of Regional OSHA Offices is set forth at Appendix 26.

WORKERS COMPENSATION

When an employee suffers a work-related injury or illness, and as a result becomes disabled and unable to work, he or she may be entitled to receive certain benefits under a system known as workers compensation. The Federal government and every state administers some type of workers compensation program according to its own statutory scheme.

A Directory of State Workers' Compensation Boards is set forth at Appendix 27.

In the majority of states, workers compensation coverage is mandatory. Employers who fail to maintain the required insurance may be sued by the employee, and are liable for damages. Depending on the jurisdiction, non-complying employers may be further penalized.

In a minority of jurisdictions, workers compensation coverage is elective, i.e., the employer may choose to reject the workers compensation system. However, if an injured employee brings a suit for damages, the employer cannot assert the three common law defenses of contributory negligence, assumption of risk, or fellow servant negligence doctrines.

THE FAMILY AND MEDICAL LEAVE ACT

The federally mandated Family and Medical Leave Act (FMLA) became effective in August 1993. It provides that employees in companies with 50 employees or more have the right to 12 weeks of unpaid leave in certain situations, such as:

1. Following the birth or adoption of a child, with 30 days advance oral or written notice, unless an emergency arises making advance notice impossible, in which case the employee must notify the employer as soon as possible;

2. To recover from a serious illness; or

3. To care for a seriously ill family member.

In addition, the FMLA provides that the returning employee be placed in the same or an equivalent job, which is defined as one with the same rate of pay, benefits, and conditions of employment, including duties and responsibilities substantially similar to the previous position.

The leave permitted under the FMLA does not have to be taken all at once. For example, it can be used to shorten the workweek for the employee who does not want to work full time following the birth of a child. Although companies are not required to pay employees who take leave, they may require or allow employees to apply any paid vacation and sick leave for which they are eligible to the 12 weeks permitted under the FMLA. In addition, state laws that grant rights greater than the FMLA supersede the statute.

Many businesses are concerned that employees seeking to take an unpaid vacation will simply claim to be seriously ill. However, the FMLA has addressed that possibility by defining serious illness as one which requires at least one overnight stay in a hospital or continuing treatment by or under the supervision of a health care worker.

Employers are required to post a notice approved by the Secretary of Labor explaining an employee rights and responsibilities under the FMLA. An employer that willfully violates this posting requirement may be fined up to $100 for each separate offense. Also, employers must inform employees of their rights and responsibilities under the FMLA. This includes giving specific written information on what is required of the employee and what might happen in certain circumstances, such as if the employee fails to return to work after FMLA leave.

THE EMPLOYEE RIGHT TO PRIVACY IN THE WORKPLACE

Computer Use

The advent of computer technology was accompanied by a number of concerns over privacy rights in the workplace, as set forth below.

E-Mail

Much of today's communication takes place through the use of a computer. For example, many workers have access to a computer through which they can send electronic messages—commonly referred to as e-mail—to another computer user.

Whether or not an employee can expect privacy of their e-mail depends largely on what type of system the employer utilizes. For example, e-mail sent on a public access system would not likely be intercepted by the employer. However, an employer would probably be able to access e-mail which takes place within the company internal system, and they often do. Thus, an employee that places offensive material in their e-mails could risk dismissal.

Private Files on the Computer

Employees often use their computers at work to create private files. Employees generally have a right to expect that personal files are private. This is particularly so if the employee maintains a password necessary for accessing these files. An employer who accesses an employee's private files must generally demonstrate that there was a valid business purpose for doing so.

Telephone Use

Employers are generally entitled to monitor business-related telephone calls which are placed to or from the business. Such monitoring is often undertaken so that the quality of service rendered by employees in customer service positions can be monitored.

The Electronic Communications Privacy Act (ECPA) which was originally enacted to regulate wiretapping, also put restrictions on the employer's right to monitor employee phone calls, as set forth below. For example, if a telephone line is being monitored for business reasons, and a personal call comes through to an employee, the employer must disconnect. However, if the employee has consented to the monitoring of personal calls, the employer does not have to disconnect. Some states require that consent must be given by both the employee and the other party to the call in order to permit monitoring by the employer.

Voice Mail

Voice mail messaging has become commonplace. It appears that the ECPA also provides some protection to employees who have voice mail systems. The ECPA provides that an employer may be held liable if it obtains, reads, discloses, deletes or prevents access to an employee's voice mail messages that are in electronic storage.

EQUAL OPPORTUNITY LAWS

There are a number of federal laws which prohibit discrimination in the workplace. Different types of employers are subject to different laws. Private employers, as well as state and local governments and public or private educational institutions, employment agencies, labor unions, and apprentice programs are subject to the equal opportunity laws listed below. Suspected violations should be reported to:

The U.S. Equal Employment Opportunity Commission (EEOC)
1801 L Street, N.W.
Washington, DC 20507.
Telephone: 1-800-669-EEOC
(TDD): 1-800-800-3302 (for hearing impaired)

A Directory of EEOC Offices is set forth at Appendix 28.

Title VII of the Civil Rights Act

Title VII of the Civil Rights Act of 1964, as amended, prohibits discrimination in hiring, promotion, discharge, pay, fringe benefits, and other aspects of employment, on the basis of race, color, religion, sex, or national origin. Most private employers, state and local governments, educational institutions, employment agencies, and labor organizations are subject to Title VII, which covers both current employees and job applicants.

The Pregnancy Discrimination Act of 1978

The Pregnancy Discrimination Act of 1978 is an amendment to Title VII. Discrimination on the basis of pregnancy, childbirth or a related medical condition constitutes unlawful sex discrimination under Title VII. Women affected by pregnancy or related conditions must be treated in the same manner as other applicants or employees with similar abilities or limitations. A written or unwritten employment policy or practice that excludes applicants or employees because of pregnancy, childbirth or related medical conditions from employment is a *prima facie* violation of Title VII.

An employer cannot refuse to hire a woman because of her pregnancy-related condition as long as she is able to perform the major functions of her job. An employer cannot refuse to hire her because of its prejudices against pregnant workers or the prejudices of co-workers, clients or customers. If an employee is temporarily unable to perform her job due to pregnancy, the employer must treat her the same as any other temporarily disabled employee; for example, by providing modified tasks, alternative assignments, disability leave or leave without pay.

Pregnant employees must be permitted to work as long as they are able to perform their jobs. If an employee has been absent from work as a result of a pregnancy-related condition and recovers, her employer may not require her to remain on leave until the baby's birth. In addition, an employer may not have a rule that prohibits an employee from returning to work for a predetermined length of time after childbirth.

Age Discrimination

The Age Discrimination in Employment Act of 1967 (ADEA), as amended, prohibits discrimination in hiring, promotion, discharge, compensation, terms, conditions, or privileges of employment for persons aged 40 and over. Most private employers, state and local governments, educational institutions, employment agencies and labor organizations are subject to the ADEA, which covers both current employees and job applicants.

The Equal Pay Act

The Equal Pay Act of 1963, as amended, prohibits sex discrimination in payment of wages to women and men who perform substantially equal work in the same establishment. Most private employers are subject to this act, which covers both current employees and job applicants. Although Title VII of the Civil Rights Act also prohibits discrimination in pay based on sex, the Equal Pay Act serves to cover employers who may not be subject to Title VII due to the size of the company.

The Americans with Disabilities Act

The Americans with Disabilities Act of 1990 (ADA), as amended, prohibits discrimination in all employment practices, including job application procedures, hiring, firing, compensation, advancement, and other terms and conditions of employment and related activities. Most private employers, state and local governments, educational institutions, employment agencies, and labor organizations are subject to the ADA.

Persons covered under the ADA are defined as qualified individuals with disabilities. In addition, persons who are discriminated against because they know, are associated with, or are related to a disabled individual are also protected. To be qualified, the person must meet the requirements of the position and be able to perform the essential functions of the position, with or without reasonable accommodation.

A disabled person is defined as a person who has a physical or mental impairment that substantially limits one or more major life activities or a record of such an impairment, or one who is regarded as having such an impairment. Covered infirmities range from paraplegia to AIDS. Minor impairments would not likely be included under the ADA.

As of July 26, 1992, companies with 25 or more employees were required to provide reasonable accommodations to qualified applicants and employees with disabilities. Businesses with 15 to 24 employees were required to comply by July 26, 1994.

In addition to employment-related concerns, businesses which serve the public, such as restaurants, hotels, theaters, and department stores, are also subject to the ADA. Such businesses must make sure their facilities are accessible to the impaired, for example, by widening doorways and installing ramps for wheelchair bound individuals.

Remedies are available to the private individual who encounters violations of the ADA. A lawsuit can be brought by an individual to stop any discriminatory practices. The Attorney General's office is also authorized to bring lawsuits in cases of general public importance. The Attorney General may seek monetary damages and stiff civil penalties, which may not exceed $50,000 for a first violation and $100,000 for any subsequent violation.

Information and ideas concerning modifications under the ADA can be gathered by contacting the various groups that represent the disabled. Information about the requirements affecting public services and accommodations can be obtained from the following office:

> Office on the Americans with Disabilities Act
> Civil Rights Division
> U.S. Department of Justice
> P.O. Box 66118
> Washington, DC 20035-6118
> Telephone: 202-514-0301
> (TDD) 202-514-0381/0383 (for hearing impaired)

The Rehabilitation Act

Section 503 of the Rehabilitation Act of 1973, as amended, prohibits job discrimination because of handicaps. Section 503 also requires affirmative action by the employer to employ and advance qualified individuals with handicaps who, with reasonable accommodation, can perform the essential functions of a job.

Employers with Federal Contracts or Subcontracts

Employers holding federal contracts or subcontracts are subject to the equal opportunity laws listed above. Suspected violations by employers against applicants or employees of such companies should be reported to:

> The Office of Federal Contract Compliance Programs (OFCCP)
> Employment Standards Administration
> U.S. Department of Labor
> 200 Constitution Avenue, N.W.
> Washington DC 20210
> Telephone: 202-523-9368

STATE EMPLOYMENT DISCRIMINATION STATUTES

Many state statutes provide additional protection against employment discrimination. Some of these laws are patterned after Title VII and other federal anti-discrimination statutes, and provide similar protection to workers employed by those employers not covered under the federal statutes. Some state laws also extend protection to additional groups not covered by the federal laws.

WORKPLACE HARASSMENT

All employees are guaranteed the right to work in an environment free from unlawful workplace harassment. Workplace harassment is a form of discrimination that violates federal and state law. Title VII is the primary piece of federal legislation prohibiting employment discrimination, including workplace harassment.

Under Title VII, workplace harassment is generally defined as unwelcome or unsolicited speech or conduct based upon race, creed, sex, religion, national origin, age, color, or disability. Persons who fall into one of the foregoing categories are considered to be in a protected class under workplace harassment law.

Additional federal, state, and local laws prohibiting workplace harassment may cover other bases for employment discrimination, including harassment based on sexual orientation, marital status, political affiliation, etc.

Although the most common workplace harassment complaints involve sexual harassment, unlawful workplace harassment is not limited to sexual harassment complaints. The Equal Employment Opportunity Commission (EEOC) has taken the position that the same basic anti-harassment standards apply to all types of prohibited harassment of protected classes, whether it involves race, creed, sex, religion, national origin, age, color, or disability.

For example, ethnic slurs, so-called racial jokes, offensive or derogatory comments, or other verbal or physical conduct based on an individual's race, color or national origin constitutes unlawful harassment if the conduct creates an intimidating, hostile, or offensive working environment, or if it interferes with the individual's work performance.

The law does not prohibit actions which constitute simple teasing, offhand comments, or isolated incidents that are not serious. The conduct must be sufficiently frequent or severe to create a hostile work environment or, in the case of a supervisor, result in a tangible employment action, such as hiring, firing, promotion, or demotion. A harassment charge may also be based on retaliation for an employee opposition to discrimination, or participation in an investigation or complaint proceedings.

Examples of Unlawful Workplace Harassment

Some examples of behaviors which have been considered unlawful workplace harassment are:

1. Avoiding or excluding someone due to race, age, sex, religion, etc.

2. Using verbal insults or degrading remarks.

3. Making unwelcome jokes about disability, race, sex, etc.

4. Offensive physical contact or coercive behavior that is intended to be derogatory or intimidating, such as unwanted touching, patting, or lewd physical conduct.

5. Making insulting or threatening gestures.

6. Making unjustified and unnecessary comments about a person's work or capacity for work.

7. Making phone calls, letters or messages of any kind that are threatening, abusive or offensive.

8. Persistent following or stalking within or to and from the workplace.

9. Dismissive treatment or material expressing prejudice or stereotypes.

10. The continual exclusion of a person or group from normal conversations, work assignments, work related social activities and networks in the workplace.

11. Sexual or racial banter, crude conversation, innuendo and offensive jokes; and discriminatory use of management/supervisory power.

12. A supervisor-promised promotion if employee agrees to a sexual relationship.

13. Displaying or circulating pictures, posters, graffiti or written materials that are offensive or obscene.

Employer Duty to Prevent Workplace Harassment

Employers have a legal duty to prevent employees from being harassed and to maintain a workplace free of national origin harassment. Employers may be responsible for any on-the-job harassment by their agents and supervisory employees, regardless of whether the acts were authorized or specifically forbidden by the employer. Under certain circumstances, an employer may be responsible for the acts of non-employees who harass their employees at work.

In order to make sure your workplace is free from unlawful harassment, you should carefully monitor the workplace for potential problems and make the necessary inquires if a problem is perceived. All complaints should be investigated immediately and taken seriously. Make sure the internal complaint procedures are followed and report the matter to others who should be involved in resolving such problems, such as the human resources representative. Although a thorough investigation should take place, the confidentiality and privacy rights of all parties should be maintained to the degree possible.

Employers should also establish and enforce a policy prohibiting harassment and setting out a procedure for making complaints. Preferably, the policy and procedure should be in writing and posted in a conspicuous area in the place of employment. The policy and complaint procedure should be written in a way that will be understood by all employees in the employer's workforce. An employer should also provide every employee with a copy of the policy and complaint procedure, and redistribute it periodically. If feasible, the employer should incorporate the policy and complaint procedure into employee handbooks, and provide training to all employees to ensure that they understand their rights and responsibilities.

An employer should also encourage its employees to report harassment to management before it becomes severe or pervasive. The employer should designate the persons who will take such complaints, and ensure that these individuals are accessible to the employees. The employer should also instruct all of its supervisors to report complaints of harassment to appropriate officials, and assure employees that it will protect their confidentiality to the extent possible.

It is not appropriate to require employees to first report harassment complaints to their immediate supervisors insofar as the immediate supervisor may not be impartial. Also, in many scenarios, it is the immediate supervisor who is accused of the harassment.

Once a complaint is made, the employer must conduct a prompt, thorough, and impartial investigation of the complaint and undertake swift and appropriate corrective action in order to fulfill its responsibility to effectively prevent and correct harassment. Due care also requires the employer to address complaints made outside of the official complaint procedure.

TERMINATING AN EMPLOYEE

Unless there is an employment agreement for a certain term, an employer can usually discharge or lay off any of its employees, with or without cause, and with or without notice. In turn, an employee is entitled to quit their job without repercussion, absent an employment agreement. This is known as "employment at will." For example, an employer can fire an employee for cause—e.g., absenteeism or incompetence—or for reasons unrelated to the employee, such as downsizing, etc.

Although an employer basically has the right to hire and fire employees at will, the law does provide some restrictions. As discussed above, an employer cannot discriminate in making any adverse employment decision, e.g., on the basis of age, race, gender, religion, national origin, or disability. Further. an employer cannot violate any other applicable federal or state employment laws.

In order to avoid a lawsuit, many employers will negotiate certain benefits, e.g., severance pay, in return for an employee waiving their right to sue. Nevertheless, employers are generally not required by law to give severance pay unless a promise to do so was made, e.g., in writing, such as a contract or employment manual, or implied, e.g., when the employer has a long history of giving severance pay to departing employees.

CHAPTER 7:
SMALL BUSINESS INSURANCE

IN GENERAL

When starting a business, it is important to meet with an insurance agent who is knowledgeable about small business insurance needs. It is important to make sure you have adequate insurance coverage for the variety of risks involved in operating a small business. There are insurance policies available that are specifically designed to cover small businesses. In addition, your other business relationships may require you to maintain certain types of insurance coverage. For example, if you lease your office space, your landlord will usually require you to produce a certificate of insurance.

Insurance is defined as a contract the insurance policy—between the two parties whereby one party agrees to compensate the other party for losses based on certain risks in return for an agreed upon payment of a sum of money, known as a premium payment. The party who purchases the insurance policy is the insured, and the party who compensates the insured if there is a covered loss, is the insurer.

For example, a flood insurance policy on your premises will insure your property in case it should be damaged or destroyed in a flood, in which case you will be compensated for the value of the property, up to the amount of insurance you purchased, less any deductible.

Public policy requires that, in order for there to be a valid policy, the insured must have an insurable interest—i.e., a right, benefit, or advantage stemming from a property, contract, or relationship, or any liability in respect thereof, that might result in the insured being damaged or suffering a loss if the contemplated risk should occur.

The purpose of this requirement is to deter a person from taking out insurance on property or an individual with which he or she has no connection, for the purpose of gambling on—or actually causing—the destruction or demise of such property or person, in order to collect money. Despite this requirement, it is not unheard of for one with an insurable interest to cause or accelerate the demise of the insured property or person in order to collect the insurance money.

TYPES OF BUSINESS INSURANCE

Depending on the nature of your business, there will be certain risks for which it would be wise to obtain insurance. Some of the types of business-related insurance that may be considered are discussed below.

Business Interruption Insurance

Business interruption insurance is designed to cover certain specified expenses of a business while operations have been stopped due to some unforeseen situation. For example, if your business premises are damaged or destroyed by a fire, earthquake, flood, or some other unforeseen reason, certain expenses still need to be paid. These expenses may include employee payroll, taxes, utilities, and other expenses of upkeep during the time your business is being rebuilt.

Business Property Insurance

A business property policy would be required if you own the building in which your business is located. If you lease your premises, your landlord is required to provide this coverage. Your business personal property may also be covered under the policy, including your desks, chairs and equipment, etc.

Catastrophe Insurance

You should insure your premises, and your inventory, against such catastrophes as floods, fires, and earthquakes, or face a total loss should one of these events occur and destroy everything. Each such catastrophe is generally covered under its own policy, e.g., fire insurance, flood insurance, etc.

Crime Insurance

Crime insurance protects the insured from losses incurred as a result of burglary and robbery. Insurance premiums for crime insurance can be reduced if you maintain an alarm system for your business. If your business is located in a high crime area, depending on the state in which you live, you may be eligible for federal crime insurance, administered by the Federal Insurance Administration, which is a division of the Department of Housing and Urban Development (HUD).

Commercial Insurance

Commercial insurance protects and compensates parties to commercial contracts in the case of a breach of contractual obligations on the part of one of the parties.

Employer Liability Insurance

Employer liability insurance protects the employer against claims made by, or on behalf of, employees who are injured or killed during the course of employment, where such claims are not covered by worker compensation insurance.

Employment Practices Liability Coverage

Employment Practices Liability (EPL) insurance is a policy that covers risks that are not routinely covered under most business policies, such as lawsuits alleging wrongful termination or sexual harassment. This type of coverage becomes more important as the size of your business and number of your employees increases.

Employer-Provided Insurance

There are certain types of insurance applicable to the employer/employee relationship that an employer may be legally required to offer—or may voluntarily offer—its employees, as explained below.

Group Term Life Insurance

Group term life insurance is provided by an employer for a group of employees. The employee does not pay taxes on the premiums paid by the employer. There is no cash value to a group life term insurance policy.

Medical and Hospitalization Insurance

A medical and hospitalization insurance plan is one offered by an employer which covers certain specified illnesses and injuries suffered by employees. The plan can be contributory—wherein the employee contributes to the premium by deductions taken from his or her paycheck—or noncontributory.

Some of the other considerations in devising a medical and hospitalization plan include deductibles, coinsurance payments, benefit limits, and whether the covered persons will include the employee's dependents as well as the employee. The health maintenance organization plan has become popular with both employers and employees, as its costs to the employer are lower than under a major medical policy, and it offers convenience to the employee, although it does take away the individual right to choose his or her own doctor without restrictions.

Unemployment Insurance

Unemployment insurance is a form of taxation collected from the business which is used to fund unemployment payments and benefits to former employees.

Worker Compensation Insurance

Worker compensation insurance compensates employees who are injured in the course of their employment, thereby protecting the employer from having to defend lawsuits brought by such employees. Employers who do not have worker compensation insurance when required by statute are directly liable to any injured employee.

Fleet Policy Insurance

Fleet policy insurance is a type of blanket policy which covers a number of vehicles owned by the same business.

Key Man Life Insurance

Key man life insurance is purchased by the business on the life of an important or key officer or employee of the business. It is assumed that the business will suffer as a result of the loss of the particular individual thus entitling the business to the proceeds of such insurance upon his or her death.

Liability Insurance

Liability stemming from operation of your business can result in many ways. For example, if a customer is injured as a result of some dangerous or defective condition on your premises, e.g., because of a slip and fall, you may be liable for his or her injuries. In addition, if your employee, in the course of business, causes injury to a third party, you may be liable to the injured person. This could occur, for example, if your employee, while driving a company truck in the course of making a delivery, accidentally strikes a pedestrian. A comprehensive general liability policy can be purchased to cover all risks except those that are specifically enumerated as exclusions.

Excess liability coverage—i.e., liability limits over and above the maximum limits of your liability policy—is also available. Excess limits—e.g., in $500,000 increments—can usually be added to the underlying liability policy for an additional premium payment.

Malpractice Insurance

Malpractice insurance protects professionals from claims of professional malpractice brought against them. Malpractice insurance is available to many groups of professionals, such as doctors, lawyers, accountants, architects, engineers, and real estate agents.

Partnership Insurance

Partnership insurance is life insurance taken out on the lives of the partners, by the partnership, which is designed to enable the surviving partner to buy out a deceased partner's estate. As your business grows this insurance can be increased.

Product Liability Insurance

If you are in the business of selling a certain product, you could be found liable to any person who is injured as a result of the use, or foreseeable misuse, of your product.

CHAPTER 8:
BUSINESS RECORDS

MAINTAINING BUSINESS RECORDS

Keeping accurate, up-to-date records is essential to the smooth operation of any business. Applications, bank statements, bids, by-laws, charters, checks, contracts, internal and external correspondence, employment forms and employee records, expense reports, insurance documents, inventories, invoices, leases, ledgers, licenses, purchase orders, receipts, reports, requisitions, shipping documents, tax returns, and other taxation documents are some of the many records which your company may be required to keep for a specific period of time.

The importance of documenting all aspects of your business operations cannot be stressed. For example, certain records may be referred to for the purpose of assessing the progress of the company. Records may be necessary if litigation arises—for example, regarding employment matters or product liability.

In addition, if taxing authorities question any aspect of your operations, accurate and complete records will assist in satisfying their audit. Thus, it is wise to engage a professional accountant to assist you with accounting and taxation records, particularly if your business operations are complex.

The nature and complexity of the records necessary to effectively manage your business are largely dependent on the type and form of business you operate. This chapter discusses some of the more common business records applicable to the small business.

THE EMPLOYER IDENTIFICATION NUMBER

An Employer Identification Number (EIN)—also known as a Federal tax Identification number (TIN)—identifies your business, similar to the way a social security number identifies an individual. Although a sole proprietor may not be required to obtain an EIN in order to do business, there are advantages to having one. For example, it is preferable to give out your EIN when carrying out business transactions instead of your social security number, which you may want to safeguard. In addition, having an EIN for your business lends more credibility to your business. An EIN is required under certain circumstances. For example, you need an EIN if you structured your business as a partnership or corporation, or if you have employees.

You can apply for an EIN from the Internal Revenue Service by phone, fax, mail or online. There is no application fee.

An Application for Employer Identification Number (IRS Form SS-4) is set forth at Appendix 29.

ACCOUNTING RECORDS

Even though you may need a professional accountant to assist you with your accounting, the small business owner should become familiar with all of the various data and forms that can be used to periodically assess the business. In performing such analysis, the company's income statement is probably the item of primary interest because it reflects the financial condition of the business over a period of time. The income statement contains the company's gross sales, costs, and expenses and gives you information from which you can determine the best method to increase sales and decreases costs.

Other accounting records may include the balance sheet, cash flow analyses, accounts payable and receivable records, and customer account information.

COMPANY FORMATION RECORDS

Depending on the form of business you chose, certain business formation documents will have to be filed and retained. Such documents may include the certificate of incorporation, by-laws, stock certificates, partnership agreements, business registration forms, and tax identification number request forms.

DEPARTMENT OF LABOR RECORDS

The Department of Labor (DOL) oversees and administers many programs and statutory schemes concerning employee-related issues, the most well known of which are the Equal Employment Opportunity Act (EEOA), the Fair Labor Standards Act (FLSA), and the Employee Retirement Income Security Act (ERISA). To comply with many of the DOL regulations, employers are required to maintain on file numerous forms concerning their employees.

EMPLOYEE RECORDS

Unless you have few or no employees, there are many employee-related documents you will need to create and keep on file in addition to those required by the DOL. For example, you will probably have some sort of employee handbook advising employees about such matters as their rights and responsibilities, holidays, benefits, and the merit evaluation process.

In addition, you may have employment contracts, payroll information, job applications, resumes, and a variety of other employee-related documentation. It is important to keep this information, even after a particular employee departs, in case employment litigation arises. Accurate and complete documentation of your relationship with your employees will assist you in defending any such action.

OSHA RECORDS

As discussed in Chapter 6, employers are responsible for maintaining a safe and healthy workplace for their employees. This requirement is overseen by The Occupational Safety and Health Administration (OSHA). Under the Occupational Safety and Health Act, employers are required to report to OSHA concerning compliance with various prescribed standards of safety and health, entailing additional paperwork for the small business owner.

Although the OSHA records are relatively simple, they are quite important. The required self-reporting documents include a summary and log of occupational injuries and illnesses, which must be filed annually, and a supplemental report describing each incident in detail.

PRODUCT TESTING RECORDS

If you are in the business of manufacturing and distributing products, you must be concerned with keeping records on testing procedures and outcomes. In the event of litigation, these records can be problematic should the testing reports reflect a potential problem related to the subject of the lawsuit.

For example, if a toy truck designed for children aged five and under was tested, and the results showed that, under certain circumstances, small parts of the truck would loosen, those records could be used to support a product liability lawsuit based on a claim that a child choked on one of those small parts. Because the hazard was foreseeable, and the company had prior knowledge of the hazard, it could be found liable for manufacturing and distributing a hazardous product.

TAX RECORDS

As you probably already know from your experience as an individual taxpayer, you cannot avoid Uncle Sam. The Internal Revenue Service, as well as many of the state taxing authorities, require a variety of forms to be filled out and submitted on a timely basis. The consequences of not properly filing the required paperwork with the federal and state taxing authorities can be costly.

BAR CODES

The Uniform Code Council, Inc., a nongovernment agency, assigns a manufacturer's ID code for the purposes of bar coding. Many stores require bar coding on the packaged products they sell. For additional information concerning a bar code for your small business, contact:

The Uniform Code Council, Inc.
P.O. Box 1244
Dayton, Ohio 45401
Telephone: 513-435-3870.

INSURANCE RECORDS

Depending on the type of business you are engaged in, insurance contracts and other documents will compose a large part of your business files. It is important to create a file to keep copies of your insurance policies in safe place, categorized by type of policy. Also retain proof of insurance premium payments. Routinely review your insurance coverage to make sure you are adequately covered for all contingencies. The various types of small business insurance policies are discussed more fully in Chapter 7 of this Almanac.

CHAPTER 9:
MARKETING YOUR BUSINESS

IN GENERAL

The goal of every business is to make a profit on the sale of its product or service to the public. In order to do so, the public has to be made aware of the existence of that product or service. You can have the best product in the world, but if nobody knows it exists, you won't earn a dime. Exposing your product or service is accomplished through a process known as marketing. Business growth will be influenced by how well the small business owner can plan and execute a marketing program.

Marketing involves the promotion and advertising of your product or service to existing and prospective buyers and users. In order to reach and capture the largest and most profitable share of your potential market, a comprehensive marketing plan should be prepared.

Marketing is the small business owner's most important organizing tool. There are four basic aspects of marketing, often called the "four Ps":

1. Product: The item or service you sell.

2. Price: The amount you charge for your product or service.

3. Promote: The ways you inform your market as to who, what and where you are.

4. Provide: The channels you use to take the product to the customer.

YOUR BUSINESS NAME

The name of your business should be easy to remember and accurately represent what your business is all about. It should be interesting, simple to pronounce, and promote a positive image. You should not choose a name that can be confused with a similar business, or that can suggest a negative visual image. You should also design a memorable logo for your business, that can be printed on your stationery, business cards, packaging and promotional items, etc.

DEFINING YOUR MARKET

Marketing encompasses much more than just advertising or selling. For example, a major part of marketing involves researching your customer base. You should define your target audience; their financial capabilities; and their needs and desires. You must determine a customer profile and the geographic size of the market. This is the general market potential. Knowing the number and strength of your competitors, and then estimating the share of business you will take from them, will give you the market potential specific to your enterprise.

The first step is to determine who will be the primary purchasers and users of your product or service—i.e., your market. Your analysis should include people who already need and use your specific product or service, as well as potential customers. You should analyze that group even further, breaking it down into smaller market segments, so that you can determine which particular group is most profitable for you and to whom most of your efforts should be directed.

For example, your hair salon may have a primarily female market. It would be difficult and cost prohibitive to market your hair salon to all females; therefore, you must narrow your market down to your most favorable customer base. Your first step in this process would be to conduct a market analysis by categorizing and identifying your customers according to like characteristics, such as age.

The results may indicate that your customer base is 20% under 25, 20% over 45, and that 60% of your customers fall into the 25 to 45 range. Thus, it will be the market consisting of females between the ages of 25 to 45 to whom you should most aggressively promote and advertise your hair salon services.

You can break your market segment down even further by comparing other available data, such as income level and profession. You may thus discover that your most profitable market segment consists of career women aged 25 to 45 who earn over $75,000 per year. You can use this information to direct your marketing efforts at the clientele who will earn you the most profit.

MARKET PENETRATION

Once you have defined your most profitable market, you must then determine how to capture the largest portion of that group. In the example of the hair salon discussed above, efforts to penetrate the market might include mailing flyers to the homes and offices of women who fit the profile and advertising in publications that would most likely include that demographic group in their readership. You may also be able to get some free advertising by sending press releases concerning your new business to the local newspapers.

Another approach is to ask your existing customers for referrals, as it is likely that they have friends and co-workers who fall in the same general category. Think of additional services you can offer that might appeal to your specific market, such as lunch-time or after-work specials for the career woman customer.

Use your own personal experience to think like the customer and to determine what products or services would attract the most people. Distribute free samples. Employ questionnaires to find out your customers' thoughts, opinions, and needs. Use this information to determine what they liked or disliked about your product or service—e.g., packaging, efficiency, etc. Try to accommodate their suggestions wherever possible, particularly when there is a consensus about a particular idea.

PROMOTIONAL ITEMS

Promotional items on which your company logo and telephone number are imprinted may be effective marketing tools. These items serve to establish name recognition and easy access. The more useful the item you distribute the better, since junk items would likely be thrown in the garbage. Popular and cost-effective promotional items include calendars, memo pads, pens, refrigerator magnets, and key chains.

KNOW YOUR COMPETITION

You should have already determined the number of similar businesses in your area before you established your location. Depending on the type of business you operate, carefully examine your competition. If you operate a service business or a retail store, visit a competitor's establishment, sample the product or service, and observe the staff. Try and find out who your competitor's customers are and what satisfies them.

Determine whether your competitor offers any additional services that you have overlooked, such as credit, free delivery, or convenient parking facilities. Analyze their advertisements. Consider whether your prices are competitive. Sometimes, price will be the only difference between you and your competitor, where products or services are substantially similar.

You must give the customers what they want or they will go elsewhere. Thus, find out what your competitors are not doing that you can do, or what they are doing that you can do better, to attract additional customers. If they have a particular marketing scheme that appears to be working, learn from it and adapt it for your own business.

REVIEW YOUR MARKETING PLAN REGULARLY

You must set goals for your company, both long and short-term. In this way, you will be able to see if you are progressing, regressing, or stagnating. Regularly review your marketing plan to see if it is working or if it needs to be modified. Determine whether your customer base is expanding and if you are earning profits.

Keep a close watch on your competitors, and find out if any new, similar operations have opened in your vicinity. Keep abreast of any new developments or trends that affect your business that may increase sales and profits. A great deal of helpful information and advice can be gathered by contacting the trade association for your particular business.

ADVERTISING

Depending on your budget and objectives, there are a number of media outlets you can use to advertise your goods and services, including: (i) network and cable television; (ii) radio; (iii) print media, such as newspapers and magazines; (iv) telephone books; (v) direct mail; and (vi) the Internet.

Stick with whatever works the best for your business. If direct mail brings in the most business, don't waste your money on radio spots. You can also try to generate interest in—and free publicity for—your business by sending "press releases" to local newspapers.

THE ONLINE MARKETPLACE

Selling Your Goods and Services Online

E-commerce refers to the sale of a company's goods and services online. E-commerce is a rapidly expanding way of doing business. It allows a small business to compete in the international marketplace without excessive costs. Many businesses have turned to the Internet to market their products. Online retail marketing is experiencing about 200 percent annual growth and online traffic doubles every 100 days. There are currently over 250 million people with Internet access, many of whom purchase goods and services online. Thus, the small business owner should carefully consider whether it is to their advantage to establish a website to sell the company's goods and services online.

Doing business on the Internet is becoming more attractive to the small business, which can now maintain and design an effective website, reach a wider market, and transact business and accept credit cards online for a relatively low cost. However, before you set up your online business, you should make sure you undertake a cost/benefit analysis.

For example, consider all of the costs involved in selling your products and services online, including shipping and handling costs; website design and upkeep; and monthly hosting fees, etc. Determine whether your potential sales will cover the monthly costs and provide you with a profit that is worth the effort.

Establishing Your Website

Whether or not you plan to sell your goods and services online, establishing a website gives you the opportunity to promote your business to a broader audience, increasing your potential customer base. Your website is all about self-promotion. You can include your website address on your stationery, business cards and promotional materials.

You have the option of designing your website "in-house" if you have an employee who has experience with website design, or hiring an independent professional website designer to set up your company website. If you decide to hire a professional website designer, you should have a written agreement that sets forth the services the designer will provide and the costs associated with setting up, maintaining, and updating the website.

If you decide to create your own website, there are software programs that can guide you through the process, even if you have little or no experience in web design. However, if your website is going to include any advanced features, it is advisable to obtain the services of an experienced professional.

Registering a Domain Name

You will need to choose and register a "domain name" for your web business. A domain name is the unique name that identifies your company. This can be your existing business name, if it is available. Most domain names end in ".com." This is known as the extension, which directly follows your company's domain name, e.g. "mycompany.com."

There are many registration services that can assist you in securing and registering your website's domain name. The registration service will also be able to tell you whether the name you choose is already taken. You can also find out if your desired domain name is free at http://www.whois.org. If the name is already taken, you will need to come up with a new domain name for your website.

It is also advisable to search the U.S. Patent & Trademark Office's database to make sure your intended name does not infringe on any existing trademarks. Once your domain name is registered, nobody else can use the name provided you continue to pay the registration fee.

Website Hosting

Running an e-commerce website can be complicated because there is a lot of competition in the electronic marketplace. Once your company's website has been designed and all of the content is in place, you need to "publish" it online. There are web-hosting services that will publish your website on the Internet for a monthly hosting fee. There are also web hosting services that offer complete services, including design of your website, however, the costs may be prohibitive for a small start-up business.

For very small businesses, one option is to sign up for a Web-based storefront, such as those offered by major servers such as Yahoo. In this way you can test putting your product online without expending large sums of money. Generally, you pay a monthly fee for this service.

Accepting Electronic Payments

Most Internet consumers use credit cards to pay for their online purchases. However, the use of debit cards—e.g., automated teller machine (ATM) cards—for online purchases is becoming increasingly more common. A debit card authorizes the seller to debit the sale amount from the consumer bank account electronically. Banks also issue debit cards that "act" as credit cards—e.g., a "debit" MasterCard. The consumer chooses whether to select the debit or credit option at the point of purchase. Either way, the funds are deducted from the consumer's bank account. The attraction of the "debit/credit" card is that it is accepted more readily for purchases.

Other types of electronic payments include cards which allow the consumer to transfer cash value to the card. These are known as "stored value cards." For example, transportation systems often offer cards that are used to gain entry instead of purchasing individual tokens and, once depleted, funds can be added to the card for continued usage. Stores now offer gift certificates in the form of credit cards. The purchaser requests an amount that is then electronically stored on the card and the recipient uses the card as they would a credit card up to the cash value of the card. The card is then discarded.

Another type of Internet-based payment system is called an "e-wallet." An e-wallet allows the consumer to establish an online account that is debited as the consumer makes on-line purchases. The consumer may use some form of stored value to establish the e-wallet account, or may set up an e-wallet account through a computer system connected to their credit or debit card account.

In order to run your web business, your bank will generally require you to obtain a special Internet Merchant Account, regardless of whether you handle transactions yourself or you have a hosting service.

Ensuring Online Security

It is important to make sure that you can offer your customers absolute security for their online transactions. One way to do so is to get a digital certificate. A digital certificate gives you a secure identity on the Internet and enables you to encrypt the messages that pass between you and your customer during transactions. Using a digital certificate to conduct transactions over the Internet is very secure provided proper security procedures are followed.

Online Marketing Potential

Doing business on the Internet allows you to track your customer base in ways not available in traditional marketing. Some companies provide information on which websites receive the most "hits"—i.e., the number of times potential customers access the site. You can also have a counter on your website which records the number of hits. Most web servers can also be configured to provide you with information on the last site your customers visited before your site, which may give you some insight into customer needs.

In addition, you can obtain referrals by linking your website with other businesses on the web that sell related products. A link is an imbedded code within your website that will take the customer to the other business's website by clicking on information related to that business, such as their name or product. These types of inter-business advertising agreements can provide an additional source of income if another business is willing to pay you to provide a link to their site on your site.

Consumer Protection Laws

The same consumer protection laws that apply to commercial activities in other media apply online.

Unfair or Deceptive Acts or Practices

The FTC Act prohibition on "unfair or deceptive acts or practices" encompasses Internet advertising, marketing and sales. The Better Business Bureau has established a Code of Online Business Practices designed to guide ethical "business to customer" conduct in electronic commerce in order to boost customer trust and confidence in online commerce.

The text of the Better Business Bureau Code of Online Business Practices is set forth at Appendix 30.

The FTC's role in protecting consumers from unfair or deceptive acts or practices encompasses advertising, marketing, and sales online, as well as the same activities in print, television, telephone and radio. Therefore, the plain language of many rules and guides applies to claims made on the Internet.

Required Disclosures

Disclosures that are required to prevent an advertisement from being misleading, to ensure that consumers receive material information about the terms of a transaction or to further public policy goals, must be clear and conspicuous. Information affecting the actual cost of an item offered on the Internet should be disclosed on the same electronic page where the advertised price is located. Advertisers should not use pop-up windows or hyperlinks to other electronic pages to display such information.

For example, where an offer advertises the availability of a rebate, where the rebate is dependent on the purchase of Internet service, the cost of the Internet service should be disclosed on the same page as the advertised price of the computer.

When using a hyperlinked disclosure, advertisers should clearly label the hyperlink so it shows the importance, nature and relevance of the information to which it links. The hyperlink should be prominent, near the claim it is qualifying, easily noticeable, and lead directly to the qualifying information. In addition, information that is significant to the advertised offer should not be buried at the end of a long web page that requires consumers to scroll past unrelated information. Consumers should not have to wander through an electronic maze to discover important conditions or limitations of an offer.

The Mail or Telephone Order Merchandise Rule

The Mail or Telephone Order Rule is enforced by the Federal Trade Commission and applies to orders placed by phone, fax or the Internet. Under the Mail or Telephone Order Merchandise Rule, all retailers, including "e-tailers"—i.e., on-line merchants—are required to ship an order within the time stated in their ads or on their website when the order is placed. A merchant must have a reasonable basis for stating that a product can be shipped within a certain time. The underlying concern is that consumers will lose confidence in the electronic marketplace if on-line merchants fail to timely ship merchandise ordered on the Internet.

If the website doesn't clearly and prominently state the shipment period, the merchant must have a reasonable basis for believing that they can ship within 30 days. If the merchant cannot ship within the promised time—or within 30 days if no shipping date is promised—the merchant must notify the consumer of the delay, provide a revised shipment date and explain the consumer's right to cancel and get a full and prompt refund.

For definite delays of up to 30 days, the merchant may treat the consumer's silence as an agreement to the delay. But for longer or indefinite delays, and second and subsequent delays, the merchant must get the consumer written, electronic or verbal consent to the delay. If the consumer does not agree, the merchant must promptly refund all the money the consumer paid whether or not a request was made.

The merchant has the right to cancel orders that he or she is unable to fill in a timely manner, but the merchant must promptly notify the consumer of the decision and make a prompt refund. If a merchant is unexpectedly overwhelmed with orders, the merchant can change their shipment promises up to the point the consumer places the order, if the merchant reasonably believes it can ship by the new date. The updated information overrides previous promises and reduces the merchant's need to send delay notices. However, the consumer must be alerted to the new shipment date prior to taking the order. Be sure to tell your customer the new shipment date before you take the order.

The Federal Trade Commission took action against seven "e-tailers" who violated the Mail or Telephone Merchandise Rule, alleging that the e-tailers missed shipment deadlines for many holiday customers, failed to notify the consumers of the delays, and continued to promise timely deliveries even when huge backlogs of orders made it unlikely that the current orders would ship on time. In addition, some e-tailers cashed their customer's money orders and checks shortly after the orders were placed, long before the shipments were made.

As a result of the FTC action, the e-tailers agreed to pay more than $1.5 million in civil penalties and consumer damages, and to abide by the FTC's Mail or Telephone Order Merchandise Rule in all future transactions.

The Telemarketing Sales Rule

Direct mail solicitations generally refer to promotional materials that consumers receive through traditional mail. With technological advances, however, these kinds of solicitations have moved online. Although the FTC's Telemarketing Sales Rule applies largely to telemarketing calls from business-to-consumer, it also applies to telephone calls the consumer places in response to a "direct mail" advertisement.

As with direct mail sent by traditional means, e-mail can convey the false impression that the recipient has been selected for an offer not available to the general public. That impression may be exploited in a telemarketing call, particularly if the direct mail piece omits important information about the products or services offered. Therefore, if an e-mail invites consumers to telephone the seller to purchase goods or services, the phone call is subject to the Telemarketing Sales Rule.

Nevertheless, not all online advertisements are considered "direct mail" solicitations. Telephone calls placed in response to general ads that do not appear to "specially select" the consumer would generally be exempt from the Telemarketing Sales Rule.

The Appliance Labeling Rule

On-line merchants that sell home appliances may be required to observe the FTC Appliance Labeling Rule which requires manufacturers of certain appliances to affix yellow-and-black EnergyGuide labels to their appliances. It also requires appliance retailers to leave the labels in place. The labels give consumers information about the energy efficiency of competing models of appliances, and enable them to factor the cost of operating an appliance into their buying decisions.

Consumers who purchase appliances through a website or catalog never come face-to-face with EnergyGuide labels. To ensure that these consumers have access to the energy efficiency information on the EnergyGuide labels before they buy, the FTC requires merchants to post the information on their websites.

The FTC's labeling and disclosure requirements apply to:

1. refrigerators, freezers, dishwashers, and clothes washers;

2. water heaters, furnaces, and boilers;

3. central air conditioners, room air conditioners, and heat pumps; and

4. pool heaters.

Dealers who sell covered appliances online or through a catalog must disclose:

1. The capacity of the particular model.

2. For refrigerators, freezers, dishwashers, clothes washers and water heaters, the model's estimated annual energy consumption.

3. For air conditioners, heat pumps, furnaces, boilers and pool heaters, the energy efficiency rating.

4. The range of estimated annual energy consumption or energy efficiency ratings of comparable appliances.

The Children's Online Privacy Protection Act

The Children's Online Privacy Protection Act (COPPA) and the FTC's implementing Rule took effect April 21, 2000. The primary goal of the Act and the Rule is to place parents in control over what information is collected from their children online. The COPPA Rule applies to operators of commercial websites and online services directed to children under 13 that collect personal information from children, and operators of general audience sites with actual knowledge that they are collecting information from children under 13.

Operators of these websites must:

1. post clear and comprehensive Privacy Policies on the website describing their information practices for children's personal information;

2. provide notice to parents, and with limited exceptions, obtain verifiable parental consent before collecting personal information from children;

3. give parents the choice to consent to the operator's collection and use of a child's information while prohibiting the operator from disclosing that information to third parties;

4. provide parents access to their child's personal information to review and/or have it deleted;

5. give parents the opportunity to prevent further collection or use of the information; and

6. maintain the confidentiality, security, and integrity of information they collect from children.

In addition, the Rule prohibits website operators from conditioning a child's participation in an online activity on the child's providing more information than is reasonably necessary to participate in that activity.

The Rule sets out a number of factors in determining whether a website is targeted to children, such as its subject matter, language, whether it uses animated characters, and whether advertising appearing on the site is directed to children.

The Commission will also consider empirical evidence regarding the ages of the website's visitors. These standards are very similar to those previously established for TV, radio, and print advertising.

The FTC monitors the Internet for compliance with the Rule and brings law enforcement actions where appropriate to deter violations. Parents and others can submit complaints to the FTC, and the FTC will also investigate referrals from consumer groups, industry, and approved safe harbor programs, as appropriate.

Website operators who violate the Rule could be liable for civil penalties. The level of penalties assessed may turn on a number of factors including egregiousness of the violation, e.g., the number of children involved; the amount and type of personal information collected; how the information was used; whether it was shared with third parties; and the size of the company.

Internet Auctions

Internet auctions are some of the most popular events on the web. These auctions offer millions of buyers all kinds of merchandise from places all over the world. Sellers market everything from vintage toys found in their attic to complete computer systems and more. There is certain information one must know about how an Internet auction works in order to successfully participate as a seller.

Internet auctions can be business-to-person or person-to-person. Operators of business-to-person auction sites have physical control of the merchandise being offered and accept payment for the goods. In person-to-person auctions, individual sellers or small businesses offer their items for auction directly to consumers. Generally, the seller has physical possession of the merchandise. After the auction closes, the seller is responsible for dealing directly with the highest bidder to arrange for payment and delivery.

Sellers usually auction one item at a time. In some cases, sellers offer multiple lots of the same item. These offers are known as "Dutch" or "English" auctions. At some sites, the seller may be required to sell all items at the price of the lowest successful bid. At other sites, the seller is entitled to the prices bid by each of the highest bidders.

A reserve price may be set by the seller which establishes the lowest price the seller is willing to accept. A closing time for the auction is set at which time the bidding ends and the highest bidder wins. If there are no bids that meet the reserve price, the auction closes without a successful bidder. Once the auction closes, if there is a successful bidder, the seller and buyer arrange for payment and delivery. This is generally accomplished via e-mail.

Depending on the seller's requirements, buyers are generally given several methods of payment, such as by credit or debit card, personal check, money order or COD. Some sellers agree to use an escrow service where, for a buyer-paid fee, the service accepts payment from the buyer in the form of a check, money order or credit card. The service releases the money to the seller only after the buyer receives and approves the merchandise.

The seller should make sure they provide bidders with an accurate description of the item they are selling, including all of the terms and conditions of the sale. Include photos of the item, if available. The seller should respond to any e-mails received by potential bidders concerning the item. Following a successful auction, the seller should contact the winning bidder as soon as possible to confirm the details of the sale, including method of payment and an estimated delivery date.

As set forth above, Federal law prohibits deceptive or misleading practices, including those associated with Internet auctions. Thus, the seller is obligated to accurately advertise their product, and honestly disclose the terms and conditions of the sale. The seller is prohibited from advertising false testimonials about either the seller or his or her product. The seller is also prohibited from placing fake bids during the auction in order to drive up the price. The seller must establish the minimum bid he or she is willing to accept. The seller must also state whether the buyer is obligated to pay for shipping costs. In addition, a seller cannot offer illegal goods or services on the Internet.

Once the auction closes, the seller is obligated to ship the merchandise within a certain time period and, if unable to do so, must give the buyer the opportunity to cancel the sale. The seller should also keep all relevant information concerning the transaction, including copies of all emails sent or received among the buyer, seller and auction site.

APPENDIX 1:
TWELVE CITIES WITH THE LARGEST
NUMBER OF WOMEN-OWNED BUSINESSES

CITY,STATE	NUMBER OF WOMEN-OWNED FIRMS	SALES AND RECEIPTS
NEW YORK, NY	251,057	$34,722,000
LOS ANGELES, CA	117,713	$15,701
CHICAGO, IL	68,581	$9,266,000
HOUSTON, TX	51,564	$10,632,000
SAN DIEGO, CA	32,513	$5,057,000
SAN FRANCISCO, CA	28,460	$4,688,000
DALLAS, TX	26,959	$5,940,000
PHOENIX, AZ	25,212	$4,866,000
SAN ANTONIO, TX	22,073	$4,508,000
SEATTLE, WA	19,945	$3,106,000
MIAMI, FL	19,127	$1,894,000
PHILADELPHIA, PA	18,977	$2,381,000

Source: U.S. Census Bureau Survey of Business Owners (2002-Issued January 2006)

APPENDIX 2:
INDUSTRIES ACCOUNTING FOR THE LARGEST RECEIPTS FOR WOMEN-OWNED BUSINESSES

KIND OF BUSINESS	TOTAL RECEIPTS	SUB-CATEGORY	RECEIPTS
WHOLESALE TRADE	$210,802,000	Wholesale Electronic Markets	$88,270,000
		Merchant wholesalers – durable goods	$62,021,000
		Merchant wholesalers – nondurable goods	$60,387,000
RETAIL TRADE	$149,231,000	Motor vehicle and parts dealers	$30,427,000
		Food and beverage stores	$22,401,000
		Miscellaneous store retailers	$16,748,000
MANUFACTURING	$93,312,000	Fabricated metal product manufacturing	$13,602,000
		Food manufacturing	$12,806,000
		Printing and related support activities	$6,910,000
PROFESSIONAL/SCIENTIFIC/TECHNICAL	$79,247,000	Management, scientific, and technical consulting services	$13,047,000
		Other professional, scientific, and technical services	$12,254,000

KIND OF BUSINESS	TOTAL RECEIPTS	SUB-CATEGORY	RECEIPTS
		Computer systems design and related services	$11,299,000
HEALTH CARE AND SOCIAL ASSISTANCE	$68,458,000	Ambulatory health care services	$44,947,000
		Social assistance	$14,534,000

Source: U.S. Census Bureau Survey of Business Owners (2002-Issued January 2006)

APPENDIX 3:
ELEVEN STATES WITH THE LARGEST
NUMBER OF BLACK-OWNED BUSINESSES

STATE	NUMBER OF BLACK-OWNED FIRMS	SALES AND RECEIPTS
NEW YORK	129,324	$7,525,000
CALIFORNIA	112,873	$9,767,000
FLORIDA	102,079	$5,728,000
GEORGIA	90,461	$5,665,000
TEXAS	88,769	$6,421,000
MARYLAND	69,410	$4,655,000
ILLINOIS	68,704	$4,984,000
NORTH CAROLINA	52,122	$3,549,000
MICHIGAN	44,366	$4,294,000
VIRGINIA	41,149	$3,718,000
LOUISIANA	40,243	$1,934,000

Source: U.S. Census Bureau, Survey of Business Owners (2002-Issued January 2006)

APPENDIX 4:
INDUSTRIES ACCOUNTING FOR THE
LARGEST RECEIPTS FOR BLACK-OWNED
BUSINESSES

KIND OF BUSINESS	TOTAL RECEIPTS
Retail Trade	$13,587,000
Health Care and Social Assistance	$11,828,000
Construction	$9,635,000
Professional/Scientific/Technical	$9,397,000
Administrative/Support/Waste Management	$6,448,000

Source: U.S. Census Bureau, Survey of Business Owners (2002-Issued January 2006)

APPENDIX 5:
TEN CITIES WITH THE LARGEST NUMBER
OF HISPANIC-OWNED BUSINESSES

CITY/STATE	NUMBER OF HISPANIC-OWNED FIRMS	SALES AND RECEIPTS
NEW YORK, NY	129,461	$8,667,000
LOS ANGELES, CA	84,679	$7,384,000
HOUSTON, TX	41,753	$7,580,000
MIAMI, FL	35,887	$5,717,000
SAN ANTONIO, TX	29,654	$5,438,000
EL PASO, TX	23,849	$2,983,000
HIALEAH, FL	22,932	$2,547,000
CHICAGO, IL	17,806	$2,991,000
DALLAS, TX	13,673	$2,032,000
SAN DIEGO, CA	12,941	$1,548,000

Source: U.S. Census Bureau, Survey of Business Owners (2002-Issued January 2006)

APPENDIX 6:
INDUSTRIES ACCOUNTING FOR THE
LARGEST RECEIPTS FOR
HISPANIC-OWNED BUSINESSES

KIND OF BUSINESS	TOTAL RECEIPTS
Retail Trade	$40,466,000
Wholesale Trade	$39,338,000
Construction	$31,439,000
Manufacturing	$18,002,000
Professional/Scientific/Technical	$15,011,000

Source: U.S. Census Bureau, Survey of Business Owners (2002-Issued January 2006)

APPENDIX 7:
CHARACTERISTICS OF VETERANS STARTING OR PURCHASING NEW BUSINESS ENTERPRISES

CHARACTERISTIC	SUB-CATEGORY	PERCENT STARTING	PERCENT PURCHASING
SERVICE-CONNECTED DISABILITY STATUS	Service-disabled	25.4%	2.6%
	Non service-disabled	16.9%	4.5%
GENDER	Male	17.5%	4.1%
	Female	20.5%	6.1%
MARITAL STATUS	Single	17.8%	4.4%
	Married	18.1%	4.4%
	Living with a Partner	22.6%	0.0%
	Legally Separated	14.3%	14.3%
	Divorced	15.1%	1.4%
AGE OF VETERAN	20 to 29	26.1%	3.8%
	30 to 39	35.9%	5.2%
	40 to 49	24.4%	11.0%
	50 to 64	14.3%	2.7%
	65 and older	1.6%	0.0%
DEPENDENTS	Dependent children	25.5%	8.3%
	No dependent children	12.7%	1.6%
EDUCATION	High school graduate	11.8%	3.6%

CHARACTERISTIC	SUB-CATEGORY	PERCENT STARTING	PERCENT PURCHASING
	One year of college	20.3%	5.0%
	Two years of college	21.8%	4.2%
	Three years of college	17.1%	5.7%
	College graduate	25.1%	5.7%
	College graduate, post graduate course(s)	18.1%	0.0%
	Post graduate degree	10.8%	10.8%
	Other	18.9%	0.0%

Source: Small Business Association, Office of Advocacy

APPENDIX 8:
NATIONAL DIRECTORY OF SMALL BUSINESS ADMINISTRATION OFFICES

STATE	ADDRESS	TELEPHONE NUMBER	FAX NUMBER	WEBSITE
ALABAMA	801 Tom Martin Drive Suite 201 Birmingham, AL 35211	205-290-7101	205-290-7404	http://www.sba.gov/al/index.html
ALASKA	510 L Street Anchorage, AK 99501-1951	907-271-4022	None Listed	http://www.sba.gov/ak/index.html
ARIZONA	2828 North Central Avenue Suite 800 Phoenix, AZ 85004-1093	602-745-7200	602-745-7210	http://www.sba.gov/az/index.html
ARKANSAS	2120 Riverfront Drive Suite 250 Little Rock, AR 72202-17956	501-324-7379	501-324-7394	http://www.sba.gov/ar/index.html

STATE	ADDRESS	TELEPHONE NUMBER	FAX NUMBER	WEBSITE
CALIFORNIA	2719 North Air Fresno Drive Suite 200 Fresno, CA 93727	559-487-5791	559-487-5636	http://www.sba.gov/ca/fresno/index.html
CALIFORNIA	330 North Brand Suite 1200 Glendale, CA 91203	818-552-3215	None listed	http://www.sba.gov/ca/la/index.html
CALIFORNIA	650 Capitol Mall Suite 7-500 Sacramento, CA 95814	916-930-3700	916-930-3737	http://www.sba.gov/ca/sacr/index.html
CALIFORNIA	550 West C Street Suite 550 San Diego, CA 92101	619-557-7250	619-557-5894	http://www.sba.gov/ca/sandiego/index.html
CALIFORNIA	455 Market Street 6th Floor San Francisco, CA 94105-24420	415-744-6820	None Listed	http://www.sba.gov/ca/sf/index.html
CALIFORNIA	200 W. Santa Ana Blvd. Suite 700 Santa Ana, CA 92701	714-550-7420	714-550-0191	http://www.sba.gov/ca/santa/index.html
COLORADO	721 19th Street Suite 426 Denver, CO 80202	303-844-2607	None Listed	http://www.sba.gov/co/index.html
CONNECTICUT	330 Main Street Second Floor Hartford, CT 06106	860-240-4700	None Listed	http://www.sba.gov/ct/index.html

STATE	ADDRESS	TELEPHONE NUMBER	FAX NUMBER	WEBSITE
DELAWARE	1007 N. Orange Street Suite 1120 Wilmington, DE 19801-1232	302-573-6294	None Listed	http://www.sba.gov/de/index.html
DISTRICT OF COLUMBIA	740 15th Street NW Suite 300 Washington, DC 20005-3544	202-272-0345	None Listed	http://www.sba.gov/dc/index.html
FLORIDA	7825 Baymeadows Way Suite 100B Jacksonville, FL 32256-7504	904-443-190	None Listed	http://www.sba.gov/fl/south/index.html
FLORIDA	100 S. Biscayne Blvd 7th Floor Miami, FL 33131	305-536-5521	305-536-5058	http://www.sba.gov/fl/north/index.html
GEORGIA	233 Peachtree Street, NE Suite 1900 Atlanta, GA 30303	404-331-0100	None Listed	http://www.sba.gov/ga/index.html
HAWAII	300 Ala Moana Blvd. Room 2-235 Box 50207 Honolulu, HI 96850	808-541-2990	808-541-2976	http://www.sba.gov/hi/index.html
IDAHO	380 East Parkcenter Blvd. Suite 330 Boise, ID 83725	208-334-1696	208-334-9353	http://www.sba.gov/id/index.html
ILLINOIS	500 W. Madison Street Suite 1250 Chicago, IL 60661-2511	312-353-4528	312-886-5688	http://www.sba.gov/il/index.html

STATE	ADDRESS	TELEPHONE NUMBER	FAX NUMBER	WEBSITE
ILLINOIS	3330 Ginger Creek Road Suite B Springfield, IL 62711	217-793-5020	217-793-5025	http://www.sba.gov/il/index.html
INDIANA	8500 Keystone Crossing Suite 400 Indianapolis, IN 46240	317-226-7272	None Listed	http://www.sba.gov/in/index.html
IOWA	210 Walnut Street Room 749 Des Moines, IA 5030-4106	515-284-4422	None Listed	http://www.sba.gov/ia/desmo/index.html
IOWA	2750 1st Avenue NE Suite 350 Cedar Rapids, IA 52402-4831	319-362-6405	None Listed	http://www.sba.gov/ia/cedar/index.html
KANSAS	271 W. 3rd Street N. Suite 2500 Wichita, KS 67202	316-269-6616	None Listed	http://www.sba.gov/ks/index.html
KENTUCKY	600 Dr. Martin Luther King Jr. Pl. Louisville, KY 40202	502-582-5971	None Listed	http://www.sba.gov/ky/index.html
LOUISIANA	365 Canal Street Suite 2820 New Orleans, LA 70130	504-589-6685	None Listed	http://www.sba.gov/la/index.html
MAINE	68 Sewall Street Room 512 Augusta, ME 04330	207-622-8274	None Listed	http://www.sba.gov/me/index.html

STATE	ADDRESS	TELEPHONE NUMBER	FAX NUMBER	WEBSITE
MARYLAND	10 South Howard Street 6th Floor Baltimore, MD 21201	410-962-4392	None Listed	http://www.sba.gov/md/index.html
MASSACHUSETTS	10 Causeway Street Room 265 Boston, MA 02222	617-565-5590	None Listed	http://www.sba.gov/ma/index.html
MICHIGAN	477 Michigan Avenue Suite 515 Detroit, MI 48226	313-226-6075	None Listed	http://www.sba.gov/mi/index.html
MINNESOTA	100 North Sixth Street Suite 210-C Minneapolis, MN 55403	612-370-2324	612-370-2303	http://www.sba.gov/mn/index.html
MISSISSIPPI	1636 Popps Ferry Road Suite 203 Biloxi, MS 39532	228-863-4449	228-864-0179	http://www.sba.gov/ms/index.html
MISSISSIPPI	210 E. Capitol Street Suite 900 Jackson, MS 39201	601-965-4378	601-965-5629	http://www.sba.gov/ms/index.html
MISSOURI	323 W. 8th Street Suite 501 Kansas City, MO 64105	816-374-6701	None Listed	http://www.sba.gov/mo/kansas/index.html
MISSOURI	200 North Broadway Suite 1500 St. Louis, MO 63102	314-539-6600	314-539-3785	http://www.sba.gov/mo/stlouis/index.html

STATE	ADDRESS	TELEPHONE NUMBER	FAX NUMBER	WEBSITE
MONTANA	10 West 15th Street Suite 1100 Helena, MT 59626	406-441-1081	406-441-1090	http://www.sba.gov/mt/index.html
NEBRASKA	11145 Mill Valley Road Omaha, NE 68154	402-221-4691	None Listed	http://www.sba.gov/ne/index.html
NEVADA	400 South 4th Street Suite 250 Las Vegas, NV 89125	702-388-6611	702-388-6469	http://www.sba.gov/nv/index.html
NEW HAMPSHIRE	55 Pleasant Street Suite 3101 Concord, NH 03301	603-225-1400	603-225-1409	http://www.sba.gov/nh/index.html
NEW JERSEY	Two Gateway Center 15th Floor Newark, NJ 07102	973-645-2434	None Listed	http://www.sba.gov/nj/index.html
NEW MEXICO	625 Silver SW Suite 320 Albuquerque, NM 87102	505-346-7909	505-346-6711	http://www.sba.gov/nm/index.html
NEW YORK	130 S. Elmwood Avenue Suite 540 Buffalo, NY 14202	716-551-4301	716-551-4418	http://www.sba.gov/ny/buffalo/index.html
NEW YORK	26 Federal Plaza Suite 3100 New York, NY 10278	212-264-4354	212-264-4963	http://www.sba.gov/ny/ny/index.html

STATE	ADDRESS	TELEPHONE NUMBER	FAX NUMBER	WEBSITE
NEW YORK	401 S. Salina Street 5th Floor Syracuse, NY 13202	315-471-9393	315-471-9288	http://www.sba.gov/ny/syracuse/index.html
NORTH CAROLINA	6302 Fairview Road Suite 300 Charlotte, NC 28210	704-344-6563	704-344-6769	http://www.sba.gov/nc/index.html
NORTH DAKOTA	653 Second Avenue N. Fargo, ND 58108	701-237-5771	None Listed	http://www.sba.gov/nd/index.html
OHIO	1350 Euclid Avenue Suite 211 Cleveland, OH 44115	216-522-4180	216-522-2038	http://www.sba.gov/oh/cleveland/index.html
OHIO	401 N. Front Street Suite 200 Columbus, OH 43215	614-469-6860	None Listed	http://www.sba.gov/oh/columbus/index.html
OKLAHOMA	301 NW 6th Street Oklahoma City, OK 73102	405-609-8000	None Listed	http://www.sba.gov/ok/index.html
OREGON	601 SW Second Avenue Suite 950 Portland, OR 97204-3192	503-326-2682	503-326-2808	http://www.sba.gov/or/index.html
PENNSYLVANIA	900 Market Street 5th Floor Philadelphia, PA 19107	215-580-2SBA	215-580-2722	http://www.sba.gov/pa/phil/index.html

STATE	ADDRESS	TELEPHONE NUMBER	FAX NUMBER	WEBSITE
PENNSYLVANIA	411 Seventh Avenue Suite 1450 Pittsburgh, PA 15219	412-395-6560	None Listed	http://www.sba.gov/pa/pitt/index.html
RHODE ISLAND	380 Westminster Street Room 511 Providence, RI 02903	401-528-4561	None Listed	http://www.sba.gov/ri/index.html
SOUTH CAROLINA	1835 Assembly Street Room 1425 Columbia, SC 29201	803-765-5377	803-765-5962	http://www.sba.gov/sc/index.html
SOUTH DAKOTA	2329 N. Career Avenue Suite 105 Sioux Falls, SD 57107	605-330-4243	605-330-4215	http://www.sba.gov/sd/index.html
TENNESSEE	50 Vantage Way Suite 201 Nashville, TN 37228	615-736-5881	615-736-7232	http://www.sba.gov/tn/index.html
TEXAS	4300 Amon Carter Blvd. Suite 114 Fort Worth, TX 76155	817-684-5500	817-684-5516	http://www.sba.gov/tx/dallas/index.html
TEXAS	10737 Gateway West El Paso, TX 79935	915-633-7001	915-633-7005	http://www.sba.gov/tx/elpaso/index.html
TEXAS	222 East Van Buren Street Suite 500 Harlingen, TX 78550	956-427-8533	None Listed	http://www.sba.gov/tx/harlingen/index.html

STATE	ADDRESS	TELEPHONE NUMBER	FAX NUMBER	WEBSITE
TEXAS	8701 S. Gessner Drive Suite 1200 Houston, TX 77074	713-773-6500	713-773-6550	http://www.sba.gov/tx/hous/index.html
TEXAS	1205 Texas Avenue Room 408 Lubbock, TX 79401-2693	806-472-7462	806-472-7487	http://www.sba.gov/tx/lubbock/index.html
TEXAS	17319 San Pedro Suite 200 San Antonio, TX 78232-1411	210-403-5900	210-403-5936	http://www.sba.gov/tx/sanantonio/index.html
UTAH	125 South State Street Room 2227 Salt Lake City, UT 84138	801-524-3209	None Listed	http://www.sba.gov/ut/index.html
VERMONT	87 State Street Room 205 Montpelier, VT 05601	802-828-4422	None Listed	http://www.sba.gov/vt/index.html
VIRGINIA	400 North 8th Street Suite 1150 Richmond, VA 23240-0126	804-771-2400	804-771-2764	http://www.sba.gov/va/index.html
WASHINGTON	2401 Fourth Avenue Suite 450 Seattle, WA 98121	206-553-7310	None Listed	http://www.sba.gov/wa/seattle/index.html
WASHINGTON	801 W. Riverside Avenue Suite 200 Spokane, WA 99201	509-353-2811	None Listed	http://www.sba.gov/wa/spokane/index.html

STATE	ADDRESS	TELEPHONE NUMBER	FAX NUMBER	WEBSITE
WEST VIRGINIA	320 West Pike Street Suite 330 Clarksburg, WV 26301	304-623-5631	None Listed	http://www.sba.gov/wv/index.html
WISCONSIN	740 Regent Street Suite 100 Madison, WI 53715	608-441-5263	608-441-5541	http://www.sba.gov/wi/index.html
WISCONSIN	310 West Wisconsin Avenue Room 400 Milwaukee, WI 53203	414-297-3941	414-297-1377	http://www.sba.gov/wi/index.html
WYOMING	100 East B Street Casper, WY 82602-5013	307-261-6500	None Listed	http://www.sba.gov/wy/index.html

APPENDIX 9:
COMMERCIAL LEASE AGREEMENT

This Lease is made on [Date], by and between [Name of Landlord] (Landlord), with offices located at [Address of Landlord], and [Name of Tenant and Address of Tenant] (Tenant). For valuable consideration, the parties agree as follows:

ARTICLE ONE: DESCRIPTION OF PROPERTY

1. The Landlord agrees to rent to the Tenant the following commercial property:

   (a) Property Address:

   (b) Description of Property:

   (c) Square Feet:

ARTICLE TWO: LEASE TERM

2. The term of this lease will commence on [Start Date], until [End Date]. Tenant will take immediate possession of the property.

ARTICLE THREE: RENT

3. The monthly rent for the property is [Dollar Amount] per square foot for a total monthly rent of [Dollar Amount], the first payment of which is due upon execution of this lease agreement.

4. Rent is payable on the first day of each month.

5. There is a grace period of 15 days after which time a late fee in the amount of [Dollar Amount] will be assessed.

6. If Tenant fails to pay rent on time, Landlord has the right to terminate this lease agreement.

ARTICLE FOUR: CONDITION OF PROPERTY

7. Tenant has inspected the premises and has found the property to be in satisfactory condition. Tenant agrees to maintain the property in such

condition, and to return the property to Landlord, upon expiration of this Lease, in the same condition as when it was first leased by Tenant, and to be responsible for any damages sustained to the property by Tenant during the term of the lease, except for normal wear and tear.

8. Landlord agrees to be responsible for the repair and upkeep of the property exterior and Tenant agrees to be responsible for the repair and upkeep of the property interior.

ARTICLE FIVE: DEPOSITS

9. Upon execution of this lease, Tenant will deposit with Landlord the sum of [Dollar Amount], which represents a security deposit which will be returned to Tenant within 15 days after termination of the Lease, minus any amounts deducted to cover the repair of any damages sustained to the premises by Tenant, according to Article Four above.

10. Upon execution of this lease, Tenant will deposit with Landlord the sum of [Dollar Amount], which represents one additional month's rent which will be returned to Tenant within 15 days after termination of the Lease, minus any amounts deducted for rent still outstanding upon termination.

ARTICLE SIX: SERVICES/UTILITIES

11. The Landlord agrees to supply the following services and utilities to Tenant during the term of this lease: [Specify]

ARTICLE SEVEN: SUBLEASING

12. Tenant shall not sublet the property without Landlord's written consent, which shall not be unreasonably withheld.

ARTICLE EIGHT: MISCELLANEOUS PROVISIONS

13. This agreement contains the entire understanding of the parties.

14. Any modification of this agreement must be in writing and signed by all of the parties.

15. This Sublease binds and benefits both parties and any successors.

16. Additional Provisions: [Specify]

_____
Landlord

_____
Tenant

APPENDIX 10:
SUBLEASE AGREEMENT

This Lease is made on [Date], by and between [Name of Tenant] (Tenant), of [Address of Tenant], and [Name of Sub-tenant] (Sub-tenant), of [Address of Sub-tenant].

For valuable consideration, the parties agree as follows:

ARTICLE ONE: DESCRIPTION OF PROPERTY

1. The Tenant agrees to sublease to the Sub-tenant the following property:

(a) Property Address:

(b) Description of Property:

ARTICLE TWO: CURRENT TERMS AND CONDITIONS

2. The above-described property is currently leased to Tenant under the terms of the following described lease, a copy of which is attached hereto: [Describe terms and conditions of current lease and attach copy].

ARTICLE THREE: SUBLEASE TERM

3. The term of this sublease will commence on [Start Date], [End Date]. Sub-tenant will take immediate possession of the property.

ARTICLE FOUR: RENT

4. The monthly sub-rental payment for the property is [Dollar Amount] per month, the first payment of which is due upon execution of this lease agreement.

5. Rent is payable on the first day of each month.

ARTICLE FIVE: MISCELLANEOUS PROVISIONS

6. Tenant represents that the underlying lease agreement is in effect and permission to sublet this property is authorized. A copy of such permission from Landlord is attached hereto. [Attach copy of proof of permission]

7. Tenant agrees to indemnify and hold Sub-tenant harmless from any claim that may result from Tenant's failure to perform under Tenant this lease prior to execution of this Sublease.

8. Sub-tenant agrees to indemnify and hold Tenant harmless from any claim which may result from Sub-tenant's failure to perform under the this lease subsequent to execution of this Sublease.

9. Sub-tenant agrees to perform all obligations and duties of Tenant under the original lease, and sub-tenant shall receive all benefits of Tenant under the original lease.

10. Tenant agrees to remain liable to Landlord for all obligations under the terms and conditions of the original lease.

11. This agreement contains the entire understanding of the partners.

12. Any modification of this agreement must be in writing and signed by all of the partners.

13. This Sublease binds and benefits both parties and any successors.

14. Additional Provisions: [Specify]

_____

Tenant

_____

Sub-tenant

APPENDIX 11:
BUSINESS CERTIFICATE

I hereby certify that I am conducting or transacting business under the name or designation of [Company Name], at [Company Address].

My full name is [Name of Company Owner], and I reside at [Address of Owner].

IN WITNESS WHEREOF, I have made and signed this certificate on [Date].

_____

OWNER'S SIGNATURE

STATE OF

COUNTY OF

On the _____ of _____, 2006, before me personally came [Name of Company Owner], to me known to be the person described in and who executed the foregoing instrument and duly acknowledged to me that (s)he executed the same.

_____

NOTARY PUBLIC SIGNATURE

APPENDIX 12:
PARTNERSHIP AGREEMENT

This Agreement dated _____, is by and between [Partner Name and Address], [Partner Name and Address], and [Partner Name and Address].

The parties agree to carry on business as a partnership, as follows:

ARTICLE ONE: PURPOSE

1. The purpose of the partnership is [State Purpose].

ARTICLE TWO: NAME

2. The name of the partnership is [Name of Partnership].

ARTICLE THREE: TERM

3. The partnership will begin as of the date first written above, and will continue indefinitely until terminated.

4. The partnership may be terminated by a majority vote of the partners.

ARTICLE FOUR: CONTRIBUTIONS

5. Each partner will contribute the following property, services or cash to the partnership, as follows:

    (a) [Name of Partner – Describe Contribution]

    (b) [Name of Partner – Describe Contribution]

    (c) [Name of Partner – Describe Contribution]

ARTICLE FIVE: BANK ACCOUNT

6. The partnership will open and maintain a bank account in the [Name and Address of Bank].

7. Check-signing privileges are as follows:

a) Checks under $100.00 may be authorized and signed by any individual partner;

b) Checks from $100.00 to $500.00 require the authorization and signature of two partners;

c) Checks over $500.00 require the authorization and signature of all partners.

ARTICLE SIX: OWNERSHIP

8. All partners will share the profits and losses of the partnership as follows:

(a) [Name of Partner – Percentage (%)]

(b) [Name of Partner – Percentage (%)]

(c) [Name of Partner – Percentage (%)]

ARTICLE SEVEN: MANAGEMENT

9. All partners will have an equal right to manage the partnership.

10. Partnership decisions will be made by majority vote.

ARTICLE EIGHT: ACCOUNTING

11. The partnership will maintain accounting records at the following location [Specify Location].

12. Each partner will have the right to inspect such accounting records at any time.

ARTICLE NINE: WITHDRAWAL

13. Upon the withdrawal from the partnership of any partner, or the death of any partner, the partnership will continue and will be managed by the surviving partners.

ARTICLE TEN: PARTNERSHIP INTEREST

14. A partner's interest in the partnership may not be transferred, in whole or in part, to any other party.

15. Upon the withdrawal from the partnership of any partner, or upon the death of any partner, that partner's interest in the partnership shall be sold to the remaining partners, in equal shares, and the remaining partners will be required to buy that interest, the value of which will be

the departing partner's proportionate share of the total value of the partnership.

ARTICLE ELEVEN: WINDING UP

16. Upon termination of the partnership, the partners agree to distribute partnership assets in the following order:

(a) Debts of the partnership shall be paid;

(b) Income accounts shall be distributed to each partner in his or her proportionate share;

(c) Capital accounts shall be distributed to each partner in his or her proportionate share;

(d) Any remaining partnership assets shall be distributed to each partner in his or her proportionate share.

ARTICLE TWELVE: MISCELLANEOUS PROVISIONS

17. This agreement contains the entire understanding of the partners.

18. Any modification of this agreement must be in writing and signed by all of the partners.

19. This Agreement is being made in [Name of State] and shall be construed and enforced according to the laws of that state.

20. Additional Terms [specify]:

IN WITNESS WHEREOF, the parties have duly executed this Agreement as of the date first written above.

_____
[Name of Partner]

_____
[Name of Partner]

_____
[Name of Partner]

APPENDIX 13:
CERTIFICATE OF INCORPORATION

It is hereby certified that:

1. The name of the proposed corporation is: [Name of Corporation].

2. The office of the corporation is to be located in: [Address of Corporation].

3. This corporation is for the following purposes: [insert specific purposes or use all-inclusive clause as follows: To engage in any lawful activity for which corporations may be organized under the laws of the State of (Name of State)].

4. The total number of shares that the corporation shall have the authority to issue is: [Number of Authorized Shares].

5. The par value of each share of stock is: [Value of Stock].

In witness whereof, this certificate has been subscribed on [Date] by the undersigned who affirm that the statements made herein are true under the penalties of perjury.

_____
Incorporator

_____
Address

APPENDIX 14:
SECTION 1244 STOCK
DESIGNATION CLAUSE

The Board of Directors has determined that in order to attract investment in the corporation, the corporation shall be organized and managed so that it is a "Small Business Corporation" as defined in §1244(c)(1) of the Internal Revenue Code, and so that the shares issued by the corporation are §1244 Stock as defined in §1244(c)(1) of the Internal Revenue Code. Compliance with this section will enable shareholders to treat the loss on the sale or exchange of their shares as an ordinary loss on their personal income tax returns.

It is resolved, that the proper officers of the corporation are authorized to sell and issue common shares in the aggregate amount of money and other property (as a contribution to capital and as paid in surplus), which together with the aggregate amount of common shares outstanding at the time of issuance, does not exceed $1,000,000, and

It is resolved that the sale and issuance of shares shall be conducted in compliance with §1244 of the Internal Revenue Code, so that the corporation and its shareholders may obtain the benefits of §1244 of the Internal Revenue Code, and further

It is resolved that the proper officers of the corporation are directed to maintain such accounting records as are necessary so that any shareholder that experiences a loss on the transfer of common shares of the corporation may determine whether they qualify for ordinary loss deduction treatment on their personal income tax returns.

APPENDIX 15:
BUSINESS PLAN

COVER PAGE

The cover page should contain the basic information about your company, including the name, address and telephone number of the company, and the contact person. You can also include a space to input the name of the person to whom you are giving a copy of your business plan and the date sent.

PART 1: INVESTOR FUNDS

This section should discuss the type of investment being offered, e.g., stock, etc., and the total percentage of ownership that is being offered. Explain why the company is seeking additional financing, e.g., to increase manufacturing capabilities, to expand its market, etc., and show how those funds will be used. Include sections that explain the risks involved, and the potential return on the investment.

PART 2: ABOUT THE COMPANY

This section summarizes the background and goals of the company. Describe the historical background of your company, including the date of organization, legal structure, and, if incorporated, the date and state of incorporation. Discuss the product or service, and the company's track record, if any, in the particular business. Explain why this company is expected to succeed.

PART 3: ABOUT THE PRODUCT (OR SERVICE)

This section should include a detailed description of the product or service, including the costs involved, such as the costs of research and development, manufacturing, and distribution. Also discuss your pricing plans, the sales projections, and potential profits. Compare and differentiate your product or service from those already available. If your product or service is unique, explain why. Include information concerning the legal status of your product, such as patent and trademark protection.

PART 4: THE MARKET

This section should discuss all aspects of the market for the product or service. Detail the overall size and nature of the market, as well as your targeted market segment. Provide hard statistical data that indicates a growing need for your particular product or service. Discuss why the product or service your company offers will be competitive in the market, and differentiate your product or service from those of other companies in the same type of business. Describe your marketing plan, including the established methods of advertising, distribution, and sales. If your product or service is unique, explain what needs it will fulfill and why it will succeed. In addition, discuss future growth and the possible crossover into new markets.

PART 5: COMPANY MANAGEMENT AND PERSONNEL

This section should list your company's management personnel and supporting staff. Discuss each manager's background, accomplishments and experience, and how they will contribute to the success of the company, and state the level of compensation. If any manager has had prior success in the particular business, point that out as well. This section should also include an organizational chart of the various departments of your company, the key support personnel in each department, and their job descriptions.

PART 6: OWNERSHIP AND CONTROL

This section should discuss ownership and control of the company. Discuss the principal's experience in the particular field and qualifications. If applicable, include a list of the stockholders of your company and how they acquired their equity. If there is a board of directors, list the members and their relevant backgrounds.

PART 7: FINANCIAL ANALYSIS

This section should summarize the company's financial condition, including capital contributions and outstanding debt. Detail the prior use of funds, such as research and development, advertising, manufacturing and distribution costs, and working capital. Include documentation of past performance of the company.

PART 8: RISK ANALYSIS

This section should include an analysis of the risks, including the methods undertaken to reduce such risks. Outline and discuss various financial scenarios, including the worst-case and best-case scenarios.

PART 9: STRATEGIES, OBJECTIVES, AND GOALS

This section should discuss your operating plan, including your specific strategies, objectives, and short-term and long-term goals. Outline the objectives you wish to accomplish at various intervals—e.g., quarterly—and your ultimate goal. Include your financial projections for the next 5 years.

APPENDICES

The appendices may include copies of the newspaper clippings, resumes, statistical data, financial tables, etc., which support the various parts of the plan.

APPENDIX 16:
PERSONAL FINANCIAL STATEMENT
(SBA FORM 413)

U.S. SMALL BUSINESS ADMINISTRATION

PERSONAL FINANCIAL STATEMENT

As of _____ , _____

Complete this form for: (1) each proprietor, or (2) each limited partner who owns 20% or more interest and each general partner, or (3) each stockholder owning 20% or more of voting stock, or (4) any person or entity providing a guaranty on the loan.

Name	Business Phone
Residence Address	Residence Phone
City, State, & Zip Code	
Business Name of Applicant/Borrower	

ASSETS	(Omit Cents)	LIABILITIES	(Omit Cents)
Cash on hand & in Banks	$	Accounts Payable	$
Savings Accounts	$	Notes Payable to Banks and Others	$
IRA or Other Retirement Account	$	(Describe in Section 2)	
Accounts & Notes Receivable	$	Installment Account (Auto)	$
Life Insurance-Cash Surrender Value Only	$	Mo. Payments $	
(Complete Section 8)		Installment Account (Other)	$
Stocks and Bonds	$	Mo. Payments $	
(Describe in Section 3)		Loan on Life Insurance	$
Real Estate	$	Mortgages on Real Estate	$
(Describe in Section 4)		(Describe in Section 4)	
Automobile-Present Value	$	Unpaid Taxes	$
Other Personal Property	$	(Describe in Section 6)	
(Describe in Section 5)		Other Liabilities	$
Other Assets	$	(Describe in Section 7)	
(Describe in Section 5)		Total Liabilities	$
		Net Worth	$
Total	$	**Total**	$

Section 1. Source of Income		Contingent Liabilities	
Salary	$	As Endorser or Co-Maker	$
Net Investment Income	$	Legal Claims & Judgments	$
Real Estate Income	$	Provision for Federal Income Tax	$
Other Income (Describe below)*	$	Other Special Debt	$

Description of Other Income in Section 1.

*Alimony or child support payments need not be disclosed in "Other Income" unless it is desired to have such payments counted toward total income.

Section 2. Notes Payable to Banks and Others. (Use attachments if necessary. Each attachment must be identified as a part of this statement and signed.)

Name and Address of Noteholder(s)	Original Balance	Current Balance	Payment Amount	Frequency (monthly,etc.)	How Secured or Endorsed Type of Collateral

PERSONAL FINANCIAL STATEMENT

Section 3. Stocks and Bonds. (Use attachments if necessary. Each attachment must be identified as a part of this statement and signed).

Number of Shares	Name of Securities	Cost	Market Value Quotation/Exchange	Date of Quotation/Exchange	Total Value

Section 4. Real Estate Owned. (List each parcel separately. Use attachment if necessary. Each attachment must be identified as a part of this statement and signed.)

	Property A	Property B	Property C
Type of Property			
Address			
Date Purchased			
Original Cost			
Present Market Value			
Name & Address of Mortgage Holder			
Mortgage Account Number			
Mortgage Balance			
Amount of Payment per Month/Year			
Status of Mortgage			

Section 5. Other Personal Property and Other Assets. (Describe, and if any is pledged as security, state name and address of lien holder, amount of lien, terms of payment and if delinquent, describe delinquency)

Section 6. Unpaid Taxes. (Describe in detail, as to type, to whom payable, when due, amount, and to what property, if any, a tax lien attaches.)

Section 7. Other Liabilities. (Describe in detail.)

Section 8. Life Insurance Held. (Give face amount and cash surrender value of policies - name of insurance company and beneficiaries)

I authorize SBA/Lender to make inquiries as necessary to verify the accuracy of the statements made and to determine my creditworthiness. I certify the above and the statements contained in the attachments are true and accurate as of the stated date(s). These statements are made for the purpose of either obtaining a loan or guaranteeing a loan. I understand FALSE statements may result in forfeiture of benefits and possible prosecution by the U.S. Attorney General (Reference 18 U.S.C. 1001).

Signature:_____ Date:_____ Social Security Number:_____

Signature:_____ Date:_____ Social Security Number:_____

PLEASE NOTE: The estimated average burden hours for the completion of this form is 1.5 hours per response. If you have questions or comments concerning this estimate or any other aspect of this information, please contact Chief, Administrative Branch, U.S. Small Business Administration, Washington, D.C. 20416, and Clearance Officer, Paper Reduction Project (3245-0188), Office of Management and Budget, Washington, D.C. 20503. **PLEASE DO NOT SEND FORMS TO OMB.**

APPENDIX 17:
APPLICATION FOR BUSINESS LOAN
(SBA FORM 4)

OMB Approval No. 3245-0016
Expiration Date: 4/30/2008

U. S. Small Business Administration
APPLICATION FOR BUSINESS LOAN

Individual	Full Address				
Name of Applicant Business					Tax I.D. No. or SSN
Full Street Address of Business					Tel. No. (inc. Area Code)
City	County		State	Zip	Number of Employees (including subsidiaries and affiliates)
Type of Business			Date Business Established		At Time of Application _____
					If Loan is Approved _____
Bank of Business Account and Address					Subsidiaries or Affiliates _____ (Separate for above)

Use of Proceeds: (Enter Gross Dollar Amounts Rounded to the Nearest Hundreds)	Loan Requested		Loan Request
Land Acquisition		Pay off SBA Loan	
New Construction/ Expansion Repair		Pay off Bank Loan (Non SBA Associated)*	
Acquisition and/or Repair of Machinery and Equipment		Other Debt Payment (Non SBA Associated)	
Inventory Purchase		All Other	
Working Capital (including Accounts Payable)		Total Loan Requested	
Acquisition of Existing Business		Term of Loan - (Requested Mat.)	____ Yrs.

CURRENT AND PREVIOUS SBA AND OTHER GOVERNMENT DEBT: Complete the chart for the following: 1) SBA loan applications pending for the applicant or any of its affiliates; 2) Federal debt, including SBA, received by the applicant including loans that have been paid in full or charged off; 3) Federal debt (including student loans and disaster loans) borrowed by any principal of the applicant; 4) Federal debt borrowed by any other business currently or previously owned by any principal of the applicant. If there has been a loss to the government as a result of a charge off, compromise, or discharge due to bankruptcy for any of the listed debt, it must be identified below. LOSS is the outstanding principal balance of the loan that the government agency had to write off after all collection activities (including compromises) were finalized.

Name of Agency Agency Loan #	Borrower's Name	Original Amount of Loan	Date of Application	Loan Status	Outstanding Balance	$ Amount of Loss to the Gov't.
# _____		$			$	$
# _____		$			$	$

ASSISTANCE List below the name(s), occupation, and address of anyone (including the lender) who assisted in the preparation of this form and who received (or will receive) compensation from the applicant for this assistance. For any person listed, an SBA Form 159 must be completed by the applicant and listed person and submitted as part of the application. The lender must complete the "Lender's Certification" on any SBA Form 159 prior to the loan being approved.

Name and Occupation	Address	Total Fees Paid	Fees Due
Name and Occupation	Address	Total Fees Paid	Fees Due

Note: The estimated burden completing this form is 12.0 hours per response. You will not be required to respond to collection of information unless it displays a currently valid OMB approval number. Comments on the burden should be sent to the U.S. Small Business Administration, Chief, AIB, 409 3rd St., S.W., Washington, DC. 20416 and Desk Office for Small Business Administration, Office of Management and Budget, New Executive Building, room 10202 Washington, D.C. 20503. OMB Approval (3245-0016). **PLEASE DO NOT SEND FORMS TO OMB. SUBMIT COMPLETED APPLICATION TO LENDER OF CHOICE.**

SBA Form 4 (2-05) Previous Edition Obsolete

Page 1

ALL EXHIBITS MUST BE SIGNED AND DATED BY PERSON SIGNING THIS FORM

BUSINESS INDEBTEDNESS: Furnish the following information on all outstanding installment debts, contracts, notes, and mortgages payable. Indicate by an asterisk (*) items to be paid by loan proceeds and reasons for paying them. (Present balance should agree with the latest balance sheet submitted).

To Whom Payable	Original Amount	Original Date	Present Balance	Rate of Interest	Maturity Date	Monthly Payment	Security	Current or Past Due
Acct. #	$		$			$		
Acct. #	$		$			$		
Acct. #	$		$			$		
Acct. #	$		$			$		
Acct. #	$		$			$		
Acct. #	$		$			$		
Acct. #	$		$			$		
Acct. #	$		$			$		
Acct. #	$		$			$		

MANAGEMENT (Proprietor, partners, officers, directors, all holders of outstanding stock –100% of ownership must be shown.) Use separate sheet if necessary.

Name and Social Security Number And Position/Title	Complete Address	% Owned	*Military Service From To	*Sex
			Service Disabled ☐	
Race *: Amer. Ind./Alaska Native ☐ Black/Afr.-Amer.☐Asian ☐ Native Haw./Pacific Islander ☐White/Cauc. ☐			Ethnicity *Hisp./Latino ☐ Not Hisp./Latino ☐	
			Service Disabled ☐	
Race *: Amer. Ind./Alaska Native ☐ Black/Afr.-Amer.☐Asian ☐ Native Haw./Pacific Islander ☐White/Cauc. ☐			Ethnicity *Hisp./Latino ☐ Not Hisp./Latino ☐	
			Service Disabled ☐	
Race *: Amer. Ind./Alaska Native ☐ Black/Afr.-Amer.☐Asian ☐ Native Haw./Pacific Islander ☐White/Cauc. ☐			Ethnicity *Hisp./Latino ☐ Not Hisp./Latino ☐	
			Service Disabled ☐	
Race *: Amer. Ind./Alaska Native ☐ Black/Afr.-Amer.☐Asian ☐ Native Haw./Pacific Islander ☐White/Cauc. ☐			Ethnicity *Hisp./Latino ☐ Not Hisp./Latino ☐	

*This data is collected for statistical purposes only. It has no bearing on the credit decision. Disclosure is voluntary. One or more boxes for race may be selected.

THE FOLLOWING EXHIBITS MUST BE COMPLETED WHERE APPLICABLE. ALL QUESTIONS ANSWERED ARE MADE A PART OF THE APPLICATION.

For Guaranty Loans please provide an original and one copy (Photocopy is Acceptable) of the Application Form and all Exhibits to the participating Lender. For Direct Loans submit one original copy of the application and Exhibits to SBA.

1. Submit SBA Form 912 (Statement of Personal History) for each type of individual that the Form 912 requires.

2. If your collateral consists of (A) Land and Building, (B) Machinery and Equipment, (C) Furniture and Fixtures, (D) Accounts Receivable, (E) Inventory, (F) Other, please provide an itemized list that contains serial and identification numbers for all articles that had an original value of greater than $5,000. Include a legal description of Real Estate offered as collateral. Label it Exhibit A.

3. Furnish a signed current personal balance sheet (SBA Form 413 may be used for this purpose) for each stockholder (with 20% or greater ownership), partner, officer, and owner. Include the assets and liabilities of the spouse and any close relatives living in the household. Also, include your Social Security Number. The date should be the same as the most recent business financial statement. Label it Exhibit B.

4. Include the financial statements listed below: a, b, c for the last three years; also a, b, c, and d as of the same date, - current within 90 days of filing the application; and statement e, if applicable. Label it Exhibit C (Contact SBA for a referral if assistance with preparation is wanted.) **All** information must be signed and dated.

   a. Balance Sheet
   b. Profit and Loss Statement (if not available, explain why and substitute Federal income tax forms)
   c. Reconciliation of Net Worth
   d. Aging of Accounts Receivable and Payable (summary)
   e. Projection of earnings for at least one year where financial statements for the last three years are unavailable or when SBA requests them.

5. Provide a brief history of your company and a paragraph describing the expected benefits it will receive from the loan. Label it Exhibit D.

6. Provide a brief description similar to a resume of the education, technical and business background for all the people listed under Management. Label it Exhibit E.

SBA Form 4 (2-05) Previous Edition Obsolete

Page 2

7. Submit the name, addresses, tax I.D. number (EIN or SSN), and current personal balance sheet(s) of any co-signers and/or guarantors for the loan who are not otherwise affiliated with the business. Exhibit F.

8. Include a list of any machinery or equipment or other non-real estate assets to be purchased with loan proceeds and the cost of each item as quoted by the seller. Include the seller's name and address. Exhibit G.

9. Have you or any officer of your company ever been involved in bankruptcy or insolvency proceedings? If so, please provide the details as Exhibit H.
If none, check here: [ ]Yes [ ]No

10. Are you or your business involved in any pending lawsuits? If yes provide the details. Exhibit I.
If none, check here: [ ]Yes [ ]No

11. Do you or your spouse or any member of your household, or anyone who owns, manages, or directs your business or their spouses or members of their households work for the Small Business Administration, Small Business Advisory Council, SCORE or ACE, any Federal Agency, or the participating lender? If so, please provide the name and address of the person and the office where employed. Label this Exhibit J.
If none, check here: [ ]

12. Does your business, its owners or majority stockholders own or have a controlling interest in other businesses? If yes, please provide their names and the relationship with your company along with financial data requested in question 4. Label this Exhibit K.

13. Do you buy from, sell to, or use the services of any concern in which someone in your company has a significant financial interest? If yes, provide details on a separate sheet of paper labeled Exhibit L.

14. If your business is a franchise, include a copy of the franchise agreement and a copy of the FTC disclosure statement supplied to you by the Franchisor. Label this Exhibit M.

CONSTRUCTION LOANS ONLY

15. Include as a separate exhibit the estimated cost of the project and a statement of the source of any additional funds. Label this Exhibit N.

16. Provide copies of preliminary construction plans and specifications. Label this as Exhibit O. Final plans will be required prior to disbursement.

EXPORT LOANS

17. Does your business currently export, or will it start exporting, pursuant to this loan (if approved)?
Check here: [ ]Yes [ ]No

18. If you answered yes to item 17, what is your estimate of the total export sales this loan would support? $_____

19. Would you like information on Exporting?
Check here: [ ]Yes [ ]No

COUNSELING/TRAINING

20. Have you received counseling or training from SBA (e.g., SCORE, ACE, SBDC, WBC, etc.)?
Check here: [ ]Yes [ ]No

AGREEMENTS AND CERTIFICATIONS

Agreements of non-employment of SBA Personnel: I agree that if SBA approves this loan application I will not, for at least two years, hire as an employee or consultant anyone that was employed by the SBA during the one year period prior to the disbursement of the loan.

Certification: I certify:

(a) I have not paid anyone connected with the Federal Government for help in getting this loan. I also agree to report to the SBA office of the Inspector General, Washington, DC 20416 any Federal Government employee who offers, in return for any type of compensation, to help get this loan approved.

(b) All information in this application and the Exhibits are true and complete to the best of my knowledge and are submitted to SBA so SBA can decide whether to grant a loan or participate with a lending institution in a loan to me. I agree to pay for or reimburse SBA for the cost of any surveys, title or mortgage examinations, appraisals, credit reports, etc., performed by non-SBA personnel provided I have given my consent—

(c) I understand that I need not pay anybody to deal with SBA. I have read and understand SBA Form 159 which explains SBA policy on Agents and their fees and have submitted an SBA Form 159 completed by the Agent and myself for each fee covered by SBA Form 159.

(d) As consideration for any Management, Technical, and Business Development Assistance that may be provided, I waive all claims against SBA and its consultants.

(e) I authorize the SBA's Office of Inspector General to request criminal record information about me from criminal justice agencies for the purpose of determining my eligibility for programs authorized by the Small Business Act, as amended.

If you knowingly make a false statement or overvalue a security to obtain a guaranteed loan from SBA, you can be fined up to $10,000 and/or imprisoned for not more than five years under 18 USC 1001; if submitted to a Federally insured institution, under 18 USC 1014 by Imprisonment of not more than twenty years and/or a fine of not more than $1,000,000

If Applicant is a proprietor or general partner, sign below.

By: _____

If Applicant is a Corporation, sign below:

_____
Corporate Name and Seal   Date

By: _____
                  Signature of President

Attested by: _____
                  Signature of Corporate Secretary

SUBMIT COMPLETED APPLICATION TO LENDER OF CHOICE.

SBA Form 4 (2-05) Previous Edition Obsolete

APPLICANT'S CERTIFICATION

By my signature, I certify that I have read and received a copy of the "STATEMENTS REQUIRED BY LAW AND EXECUTIVE ORDER" which was attached to this application. My signature represents my agreement to comply with the approval of my loan request and to comply, whenever applicable, with the hazard insurance, lead-based paint, civil rights or other limitations in this notice.

Each Proprietor, each General Partner, each Limited Partner or Stockholder owning 20% or more, each Guarantor, and the spouse, when applicable, of each of these must sign. Each person should sign only once.

Business Name: _____

By: _____
Signature and Title   Date _____

Guarantors:

_____
Signature and Title   Date _____

_____
Signature and Title   Date _____

_____
Signature and Title   Date _____

_____
Signature and Title   Date _____

_____
Signature and Title   Date _____

_____
Signature and Title   Date _____

_____
Signature and Title   Date _____

SBA Form 4 (2-05) Previous Edition Obsolete

Page 4

PLEASE READ, DETACH, AND RETAIN FOR YOUR RECORDS
STATEMENTS REQUIRED BY LAW AND EXECUTIVE ORDER

Federal executive agencies, including the Small Business Administration (SBA), are required to withhold or limit financial assistance, to impose special conditions on approved loans, to provide special notices to applicants or borrowers and to require special reports and data from borrowers in order to comply with legislation passed by the Congress and Executive Orders issued by the President and by the provisions of various inter-agency agreements. SBA has issued regulations and procedures that implement these laws and executive orders, and they are contained in Parts 112, 113, 116, and 117, Title 13, Code of Federal Regulations Chapter 1, or Standard Operating Procedures.

Freedom of Information Act (5 U.S.C. 552)
This law provides, with some exceptions, that SBA must supply information reflected in agency files and records to a person requesting it. Information about approved loans that will be automatically released includes, among other things, statistics on our loan programs (individual borrowers are not identified in the statistics) and other information such as the names of the borrowers (and their officers, directors, stockholders or partners), the collateral pledged to secure the loan, the amount of the loan, its purpose in general terms and the maturity. Proprietary data on a borrower would not routinely be made available to third parties. All requests under this Act are to be addressed to the nearest SBA office and be identified as a Freedom of Information request.

Privacy Act (5 U.S.C. 552a)

A person can request to see or get copies of any personal information that SBA has in his or her file when that file is retrievable by individual identifiers such as name or social security numbers. Requests for information about another party may be denied unless SBA has the written permission of the individual to release the information to the requestor or unless the information is subject to disclosure under the Freedom of Information Act.

Under the provisions of the Privacy Act, you are not required to provide your social security number. Failure to provide your social security number may not affect any right, benefit or privilege to which you are entitled. Disclosures of name and other personal identifiers are, however, required for a benefit, as SBA requires an individual seeking assistance from SBA to provide it with sufficient information for it to make a character determination. In determining whether an individual is of good character, SBA considers the person's integrity, candor, and disposition toward criminal actions. In making loans pursuant to section 7(a)(6) of the Small Business Act (the Act), 15 USC Section 636(a)(6), SBA is required to have reasonable assurance that the loan is of sound value and will be repaid or that it is in the best interest of the Government to grant the assistance requested. Additionally, SBA is specifically authorized to verify your criminal history, or lack thereof, pursuant to section 7(a)(1)(B), 15 USC Section 636(a)(1)(B). Further, for all forms of assistance, SBA is authorized to make all investigations necessary to ensure that a person has not engaged in acts that violate or will violate the Act or the Small Business Investment Act, 15 USC Sections 634(b)(11) and 687(b)(a). For these purposes, you are asked to voluntarily provide your social security number to assist SBA in making a character determination and to distinguish you from other individuals with the same or similar name or other personal identifier.

The Privacy Act authorizes SBA to make certain "routine uses" of information protected by that Act. One such routine use for SBA's loan system of records is that when this information indicates a violation or potential violation of law, whether civil, criminal, or administrative in nature, SBA may refer it to the appropriate agency, whether Federal, State, local or foreign, charged with responsibility for or otherwise involved in investigation, prosecution, enforcement or prevention of such violations. Another routine use of personal information is to assist in obtaining credit bureau reports, including business credit reports on the small business borrower and consumer credit reports and scores on the principals of the small business and guarantors on the loan for purposes of originating, servicing, and liquidating small business loans and for purposes of routine periodic loan portfolio management and lender monitoring. See, 69 F.R. 58598, 58617 (and as amended from time to time) for additional background and other routine uses.

Right to Financial Privacy Act of 1978 (12 U.S.C. 3401)
This is notice to you as required by the Right of Financial Privacy Act of 1978, of SBA's access rights to financial records held by financial institutions that are or have been doing business with you or your business, including any financial institutions participating in a loan or loan guarantee. The law provides that SBA shall have a right of access to your financial records in connection with its consideration or administration of assistance to you in the form of a Government loan or loan guaranty agreement. SBA is required to provide a certificate of its compliance with the Act to a financial institution in connection with its first request for access to your financial records, after which no further certification is required for subsequent accesses. The law also provides that SBA's access rights continue for the term of any approved loan or loan guaranty agreement. No further notice to you of SBA's access rights is required during the term of any such agreement.

The law also authorizes SBA to transfer to another Government authority any financial records included in an application for a loan, or concerning an approved loan or loan guarantee, as necessary to process, service or foreclose on a loan or loan guarantee or to collect on a defaulted loan or loan guarantee. No other transfer of your financial records to another Government authority will be permitted by SBA except as required or permitted by law.

Flood Disaster Protection Act (42 U.S.C. 4011)
Regulations have been issued by the Federal Insurance Administration (FIA) and by SBA implementing this Act and its amendments. These regulations prohibit SBA from making certain loans in an FIA designated floodplain unless Federal flood insurance is purchased as a condition of the loan. Failure to maintain the required level of flood insurance makes the applicant ineligible for any future financial assistance from SBA under any program, including disaster assistance.

Executive Orders -- Floodplain Management and Wetland Protection (42 F.R. 26951 and 42 F.R. 26961)
The SBA discourages any settlement in or development of a floodplain or a wetland. This statement is to notify all SBA loan applicants that such actions are hazardous to both life and property and should be avoided. The additional cost of flood preventive construction must be considered in addition to the possible loss of all assets and investments in future floods.

Occupational Safety and Health Act (15 U.S.C. 651 et seq.)
This legislation authorizes the Occupational Safety and Health Administration in the Department of Labor to require businesses to modify facilities and procedures to protect employees or pay penalty fees. In some instances the business can be forced to cease operations or be prevented from starting operations in a new facility. Therefore, in some instances SBA may require additional information from an applicant to determine whether the business will be in compliance with OSHA regulations and allowed to operate its facility after the loan is approved and disbursed. Signing this form as borrower is a certification that the OSA requirements that apply to the borrower's business have been determined and the borrower to the best of its knowledge is in compliance.

Civil Rights Legislation
All businesses receiving SBA financial assistance must agree not to discriminate in any business practice, including employment practices and services to the public, on the basis of categories cited in 13 C.F.R., Parts 112, 113, and 117 of SBA Regulations. This includes making their goods and services available to handicapped clients or customers. All business borrowers will be required to display the "Equal Employment Opportunity Poster" prescribed by SBA.

Equal Credit Opportunity Act (15 U.S.C. 1691)
The Federal Equal Credit Opportunity Act prohibits creditors from discriminating against credit applicants on the basis of race, color, religion, national origin, sex, marital status or age (provided that the applicant has the capacity to enter into a binding contract); because all or part of the applicant's income derives from any public assistance program, or because the applicant has in good faith exercised any right under the Consumer Credit Protection Act. The Federal agency that administers compliance with this law concerning this creditor is the Federal Trade Commission, Equal Credit Opportunity, Washington, D.C. 20580.

Executive Order 11738 -- Environmental Protection (38 C.F.R. 25161)
The Executive Order charges SBA with administering its loan programs in a manner that will result in effective enforcement of the Clean Air Act, the Federal Water Pollution Act and other environmental protection legislation. SBA must, therefore, impose conditions on some loans. By acknowledging receipt of this form and presenting the application, the principals of all small businesses borrowing $100,000 or more in direct funds stipulate to the following:

1. That any facility used, or to be used, by the subject firm is not cited on the EPA list of Violating Facilities.

2. That subject firm will comply with all the requirements of Section 114 of the Clean Air Act (42 U.S.C. 7414) and Section 308 of the Water Act (33 U.S.C 1318) relating to inspection, monitoring, entry, reports and information, as well as all other requirements specified in Section 114 and Section 308 of the respective Acts, and all regulations and guidelines issued thereunder.

3. That subject firm will notify SBA of the receipt of any communication from the Director of the Environmental Protection Agency indicating that a facility utilized, or to be utilized, by subject firm is under consideration to be listed on the EPA List of Violating Facilities.

Debt Collection Act of 1982 Deficit Reduction Act of 1984 (31 U.S.C. 3701 et seq. and other titles)
These laws require SBA to aggressively collect any loan payments which become delinquent. SBA must obtain your taxpayer identification number when you apply for a loan. If you receive a loan, and do not make payments as they come due, SBA may take one or more of the following actions:

- Report the status of your loan(s) to credit bureaus
- Hire a collection agency to collect your loan
- Offset your income tax refund or other amounts due to you from the Federal Government
- Suspend or debar you or your company from doing business with the Federal Government
- Refer your loan to the Department of Justice or other attorneys for litigation
- Foreclose on collateral or take other action permitted in the loan instruments.

Immigration Reform and Control Act of 1986 (Pub. L. 99-603)
If you are an alien who was in this country illegally since before January 1, 1982, you may have been granted lawful temporary resident status by the United States Immigration and Naturalization Service pursuant to the Immigration Reform and Control Act of 1986 (Pub. L. 99-603). For five years from the date you are granted such status, you are not eligible for financial assistance from the SBA in the form of a loan or guaranty under section 7(a) of the Small Business Act unless you are disabled or a Cuban or Haitian entrant. When you sign this document, you are making the certification that the Immigration Reform and Control Act of 1986 does not apply to you, or if it does apply, more than five years have elapsed since you have been granted lawful temporary resident status pursuant to such 1986 legislation.

Lead-Based Paint Poisoning Prevention Act (42 U.S.C. 4821 et seq.)
Borrowers using SBA funds for the construction or rehabilitation of a residential structure are prohibited from using lead-based paint (as defined in SBA regulations) on all interior surfaces, whether accessible or not, and exterior surfaces, such as stairs, decks, porches, railings, windows and doors, which are readily accessible to children under 7 years of age. A "residential structure" is any home, apartment, hotel, motel, orphanage, boarding school, dormitory, day care center, extended care facility, college or other school housing, hospital, group practice or community facility and all other residential or institutional structures where persons reside.

Executive Order 12549, Debarment and Suspension (13 C.F.R. 145)

1. The prospective lower tier participant certifies, by submission of this loan application, that neither it nor its principals are presently debarred, suspended, proposed for debarment, declared ineligible, or voluntarily excluded from participation in this transaction by any Federal department or agency.

2. Where the prospective lower tier participant is unable to certify to any of the statements in this certification, such prospective participants shall attach an explanation to the loan application.

SBA Form 4 (2-05) Previous Edition Obsolete

Page 7

APPENDIX 18:
DISASTER BUSINESS LOAN APPLICATION
(SBA FORM 5)

U. S. Small Business Administration
DISASTER BUSINESS LOAN APPLICATION

OMB No. 3245-0017

FOR SBA INTERNAL USE ONLY

Physical Declaration Number		Filing Deadline Date	
Economic Injury Declaration Number		Filing Deadline Date	
FEMA Registration Number (if known)		SBA Application Number	

1. ARE YOU APPLYING FOR:

☐ **Physical Damage** -- *Indicate type of damage*

   ☐ Real Property   ☐ Business Contents

☐ **Economic Injury (EIDL)**

☐ **Military Reservist EIDL (MREIDL)**
   (complete the following)
   * Name of Essential Employee _____
   * Employee's Social Security Number _____ - ___ - _____

PLEASE PROVIDE ALL INFORMATION OR DOCUMENTATION REQUESTED IN THE ATTACHED FILING REQUIREMENTS.
* For information about these questions, see the attached Statements Required by Laws and Executive Orders.

2. ORGANIZATION TYPE

☐ Sole Proprietorship   ☐ Partnership   ☐ Limited Partnership   ☐ Limited Liability Entity

☐ Corporation   ☐ Nonprofit Organization   ☐ Trust   ☐ Other: _____

3. APPLICANT'S LEGAL NAME	4. FEDERAL E.I.N. (if applicable)

5. TRADE NAME (if different from legal name)	6. BUSINESS PHONE NUMBER (including area code)

7. MAILING ADDRESS   ☐ Business   ☐ Home   ☐ Temp   ☐ Other _____

Number, Street, and/or Post Office Box	City	County	State	Zip

8. DAMAGED PROPERTY ADDRESS(ES)
(If you need more space, attach additional sheets.)   ☐ Same as mailing address

Number and Street Name	City	County	State	Zip

9. PROVIDE THE NAME(S) OF THE INDIVIDUAL(S) TO CONTACT FOR:

☐ Loss Verification Inspection   ☐ Information necessary to process the Application

Name	Name
Telephone Number	Telephone Number

10. ALTERNATE WAY TO CONTACT YOU (ie., cell #, fax #, e-mail, etc.)

Cell # ☐ Fax # ☐ E-mail ☐ Other ☐	Cell # ☐ Fax # ☐ E-mail ☐ Other ☐

11. TYPE OF BUSINESS:	12. DATE BUSINESS ESTABLISHED:
13. UNDER CURRENT MANAGEMENT SINCE:	**14. BUSINESS PROPERTY IS:** ☐ Owned ☐ Leased
15. AMOUNT OF ESTIMATED LOSS: If unknown, enter a question mark	**16. NUMBER OF EMPLOYEES:**

17. IF YOU ARE A SOLE PROPRIETOR, ARE YOU A U.S. CITIZEN?   ☐ YES   ☐ NO

18. IF YOU HAVE ANY TYPE OF INSURANCE, PLEASE COMPLETE THE FOLLOWING:

Name of Insurance Company and Agent	
Phone Number of Insurance Agent	Policy Number

SBA Form 5 (01-05) Ref SOP 50 30

---

19. OWNERS (If you need more space attach additional sheets.)   Complete for each: 1) proprietor, or 2) limited partner who owns 20% or more interest and each general partner, or 3) stockholder or entity owning 20% or more voting stock.

Name				Title/Office	% Owned	E-mail Address		
SSN/EIN*	Marital Status	Date of Birth*	Place of Birth*	Telephone Number (including area code)				
Mailing Address				City			State	Zip
Name				Title/Office	% Owned	E-mail Address		
SSN/EIN*	Marital Status	Date of Birth*	Place of Birth*	Telephone Number (including area code)				
Mailing Address				City			State	Zip

* For information about these questions, see the attached Statements Required by Laws and Executive Orders.

20. For the applicant business and each owner listed in item 19, please respond to the following questions, providing dates and details on any question answered **YES**. (Attach an additional sheet for detailed responses.)

  a. Has the business or a listed owner ever been involved in a bankruptcy or insolvency proceeding? ☐ Yes ☐ No

  b. Does the business or a listed owner have any outstanding judgments, tax liens, or pending lawsuits against them? ☐ Yes ☐ No

  c. Has the business or a listed owner ever been convicted of a criminal offense committed during and in connection with a riot or civil disorder or ever been engaged in the production or distribution of any product or service that has been determined to be obscene by a court of competent jurisdiction? ☐ Yes ☐ No

  d. Has the business or a listed owner ever had or guaranteed a Federal loan or a Federally guaranteed loan? ☐ Yes ☐ No

  e. Is the business or a listed owner delinquent on any Federal taxes, direct or guaranteed Federal loans (SBA, FHA, VA, student, etc.), Federal contracts, Federal grants, or any child support payments? ☐ Yes ☐ No

  f. Does any owner, owner's spouse, or household member work for SBA or serve as a member of SBA's SCORE, ACE, or Advisory Council? ☐ Yes ☐ No

21. Is the applicant or any of the individuals listed in Item 19 currently, or have they <u>ever</u> been:

  a) under indictment, on parole or probation; b) charged with or arrested for any criminal offense other than a minor motor vehicle violation, including offenses which have been dismissed, discharged, or not prosecuted; or c) convicted, placed on pretrial diversion, or placed on any form of probation, including adjudication withheld pending probation, for any criminal offense other than a minor motor vehicle violation?

  ☐ Yes   ☐ No   If yes, Name _____

22. PHYSICAL DAMAGE LOANS ONLY. If your application is approved, you may be eligible for additional funds to cover the cost of mitigating measures (real property improvements or devices to minimize or protect against future damage from the same type of disaster event). It is not necessary for you to submit the description and cost estimates with the application. SBA must approve the mitigating measures before any loan increase.

  By checking this box, I am interested in having SBA consider this increase. ☐

23. If anyone assisted you in completing this application, whether you pay a fee for this service or not, that person must print and sign their name in the space below.

  Name and Address of representative (please include the individual name and their company)

  _____   _____
  (Signature of Individual)   (Print Individual Name)

  _____   _____
  (Name of Company)   Phone Number (include Area Code)

  _____   _____
  Street Address, City, State, Zip   Fee Charged or Agreed Upon

  Unless the NO box is checked, I give permission for SBA to discuss any portion of this application with the representative listed above.   NO ☐

AGREEMENTS AND CERTIFICATIONS

On behalf of the undersigned individually and for the applicant business:

  I authorize my insurance company, bank, financial institution, or other creditors to release to SBA all records and information necessary to process this application.

  I give my permission to release information in connection with this application to Federal, state, local, or private organizations that provide relief for disaster related purposes.

  I will not exclude from participating in, or deny the benefits of, or otherwise subject to discrimination under, any program or activity for which I receive Federal financial assistance from SBA, any person on grounds of age, color, handicap, marital status, national origin, race, religion, or sex.

  I will report to the SBA Office of the Inspector General, Washington, DC 20416, any Federal employee who offers, in return for compensation of any kind, to help get this loan approved. I have not paid anyone connected with the Federal government for help in getting this loan.

  All information in and submitted with this application is true and correct to the best of my knowledge. All financial statements submitted with this application fully and accurately present the financial position of the business. I have not omitted any disclosures in these financial statements. This certification also applies to any financial statements or other information submitted after this date. I understand that false statements may result in the forfeiture of benefits and possible prosecution by the U.S. Attorney General (reference 18 U.S.C. 1001 and/or 15 U.S.C. 645).

SIGNATURE		TITLE		DATE	
Sign in ink					

APPENDIX 19:
EMPLOYMENT AGREEMENT

This Agreement dated [Date], is by and between [Company Name and Address] (Company) and [Employee Name and Address] (Employee).

For valuable consideration, Company and Employee agree as follows:

ARTICLE ONE: TITLE

1. Company hereby engages the services of Employee as its [Specify Title].

ARTICLE TWO: TERM

2. Employee hereby agrees to perform services for Company in the capacity of [Title], for a one-year term beginning [Start Date] and ending [End Date].

3. This agreement may be renewed annually, for one additional year, on the same terms and conditions as contained herein, unless either party notifies the other prior to the end of the existing term, of that party's intention not to renew this agreement.

ARTICLE THREE: COMPENSATION

4. Company agrees to compensate Employee as follows:

(a) For the first year during which this agreement is in effect, Company agrees to compensate Employee for services rendered at an annual salary of [Dollar Amount].

(b) For the second year, and all succeeding years, during which this agreement is in effect, Employee shall receive an increase to Employee's then annual salary of ten percent (10%).

(c) In addition to Employee's annual salary, Employee will be entitled to an annual bonus equal to ten percent (10%) of Employee's then annual salary.

ARTICLE FOUR: JOB DESCRIPTION

5. Employee shall perform the following duties and responsibilities: [Specify duties and responsibilities]

ARTICLE FIVE: PERFORMANCE EVALUATION

6. Company will evaluate employee's performance on an annual basis to determine whether Employee's contract shall be renewed for an additional 1-year term. Such evaluation shall take place prior to the expiration of the existing term.

ARTICLE SIX: EMPLOYEE EXPENSE ACCOUNT

7. Company shall pay or reimburse Employee for all ordinary and necessary expenses incurred by Employee in performance of his or her duties under this agreement, upon submission by Employee of the appropriate expense account forms.

ARTICLE SEVEN: INSURANCE

8. Company shall purchase a term life plan insurance policy on the life of Employee in a policy amount of not less than [Dollar Amount], and shall pay all premiums due and owing on such policy. Employee shall designate the beneficiary to such policy.

9. Company shall provide Employee with medical and hospital insurance as outlined in Company's employee handbook, a copy of which is attached hereto.

ARTICLE EIGHT: VACATION AND PERSONAL LEAVE

10. Employee shall be entitled to accrue vacation and personal leave time as outlined in Company's employee handbook, a copy of which is attached hereto.

ARTICLE NINE: NOTICES

11. Any notice required to be given under this agreement shall be sent by certified mail, return receipt requested, as follows:

To Company:

[Company Name and Address]

To Employee:

[Employee Name and Address]

ARTICLE TEN: ADDITIONAL PROVISIONS

12. The waiver by either party of any term or condition of this agreement shall not constitute a waiver of any other term or condition of this agreement.

13. This agreement contains the entire understanding of the partners.

14. Any modification of this agreement must be in writing and signed by both parties.

15. This agreement is being made in [Name of State] and shall be construed and enforced according to the laws of that state.

16. Additional Terms: [Specify]

IN WITNESS WHEREOF, the parties have duly executed this agreement as of the date first written above.

_____

Employer

_____

Employee

APPENDIX 20:
EMPLOYMENT ELIGIBILITY VERIFICATION (FORM I-9)

Department of Homeland Security
U.S. Citizenship and Immigration Services

OMB No. 1615-0047; Expires 03/31/07

Employment Eligibility Verification

INSTRUCTIONS

PLEASE READ ALL INSTRUCTIONS CAREFULLY BEFORE COMPLETING THIS FORM.

Anti-Discrimination Notice. It is illegal to discriminate against any individual (other than an alien not authorized to work in the U.S.) in hiring, discharging, or recruiting or referring for a fee because of that individual's national origin or citizenship status. It is illegal to discriminate against work eligible individuals. Employers **CANNOT** specify which document(s) they will accept from an employee. The refusal to hire an individual because of a future expiration date may also constitute illegal discrimination.

Section 1- Employee. All employees, citizens and noncitizens, hired after November 6, 1986, must complete Section 1 of this form at the time of hire, which is the actual beginning of employment. **The employer is responsible for ensuring that Section 1 is timely and properly completed.**

Preparer/Translator Certification. The Preparer/Translator Certification must be completed if Section 1 is prepared by a person other than the employee. A preparer/translator may be used only when the employee is unable to complete Section 1 on his/her own. However, the employee must still sign Section 1 personally.

Section 2 - Employer. For the purpose of completing this form, the term "employer" includes those recruiters and referrers for a fee who are agricultural associations, agricultural employers or farm labor contractors.

Employers must complete Section 2 by examining evidence of identity and employment eligibility within three (3) business days of the date employment begins. If employees are authorized to work, but are unable to present the required document(s) within three business days, they must present a receipt for the application of the document(s) within three business days and the actual document(s) within ninety (90) days.†However, if employers hire individuals for a duration of less than three business days, Section 2 must be completed at the time employment begins. **Employers must record: 1)** document title; **2)** issuing authority; **3)** document number, **4)** expiration date, if any; and **5)** the date employment begins. Employers must sign and date the certification. Employees†must present original documents. Employers may, but are not required to, photocopy the document(s) presented. These photocopies may only be used for the verification process and must be retained with the I-9. **However, employers are still responsible for completing the I-9.**

Section 3 - Updating and Reverification. Employers must complete Section 3 when updating and/or reverifying the I-9. Employers must reverify employment eligibility of their employees on or before the expiration date recorded in Section 1.†Employers **CANNOT** specify which document(s) they will accept from an employee

- If an employee's name has changed at the time this form is being updated/reverified, complete Block A.

- If an employee is rehired within three (3) years of the date this form was originally completed and the employee is still eligible to be employed on the same basis as previously indicated on this form (updating), complete Block B and the signature block.

- If an employee is rehired within three (3) years of the date this form was originally completed and the employee's work authorization has expired **or** if at current employee's work authorization is about to expire (reverification), complete Block B and:

- examine any document that reflects that the employee is authorized to work in the U.S. (see List A or C),

- record the document title, document number and expiration date (if any) in Block C, and

- complete the signature block.

Photocopying and Retaining Form I-9. A blank I-9 may be reproduced, provided both sides are copied. The Instructions†must be available to all employees completing this form. Employers must retain completed I-9s for three (3) years after the date of hire or one (1) year after the date employment ends, whichever is later.

For more detailed information, you may refer to the Department of Homeland Security (DHS) Handbook for Employers, (Form M-274). You may obtain the handbook at your local U.S. Citizenship and Immigration Services (USCIS) office.

Privacy Act Notice. The authority for collecting this information is the Immigration Reform and Control Act of 1986, Pub. L. 99-603 (8 USC 1324a).

This information is for employers to verify the eligibility of individuals for employment to preclude the unlawful hiring, or recruiting or referring for a fee, of aliens who are not authorized to work in the United States.

This information will be used by employers as a record of their basis for determining eligibility of an employee to work in the United States. The form will be kept by the employer and made available for inspection by officials of the U.S. Immigration and Customs Enforcement, Department of Labor and Office of Special Counsel for Immigration Related Unfair Employment Practices.

Submission of the information required in this form is voluntary. However, an individual may not begin employment unless this form is completed, since employers are subject to civil or criminal penalties if they do not comply with the Immigration Reform and Control Act of 1986.

Reporting Burden. We try to create forms and instructions that are accurate, can be easily understood and which impose the least possible burden on you to provide us with information. Often this is difficult because some immigration laws are very complex. Accordingly, the reporting burden for this collection of information is computed as follows: **1)** learning about this form,†5 minutes; **2)** completing the form, 5 minutes; and **3)** assembling and filing (recordkeeping) the form, 5 minutes, for an average of 15 minutes per response. If you have comments regarding the accuracy of this burden estimate, or suggestions for making this form simpler, you can write to U.S. Citizenship and Immigration Services, Regulatory Management Division, 111 Massachuetts Avenue,†N.W., Washington, DC 20529. OMB No. 1615-0047.

NOTE: This is the 1991 edition of the Form I-9 that has been rebranded with a current printing date to reflect the recent transition from the INS to DHS and its components.

EMPLOYERS MUST RETAIN COMPLETED FORM I-9
PLEASE DO NOT MAIL COMPLETED FORM I-9 TO ICE OR USCIS

Form I-9 (Rev. 05/31/05)Y

Department of Homeland Security
U.S. Citizenship and Immigration Services

OMB No. 1615-0047; Expires 03/31/07

Employment Eligibility Verification

Please read instructions carefully before completing this form. The instructions must be available during completion of this form. ANTI-DISCRIMINATION NOTICE: It is illegal to discriminate against work eligible individuals. Employers CANNOT specify which document(s) they will accept from an employee. The refusal to hire an individual because of a future expiration date may also constitute illegal discrimination.

Section 1. Employee Information and Verification. To be completed and signed by employee at the time employment begins.

Print Name: Last	First	Middle Initial	Maiden Name

Address (Street Name and Number)		Apt. #	Date of Birth (month/day/year)

City	State	Zip Code	Social Security #

I am aware that federal law provides for imprisonment and/or fines for false statements or use of false documents in connection with the completion of this form.

I attest, under penalty of perjury, that I am (check one of the following):

☐ A citizen or national of the United States
☐ A Lawful Permanent Resident (Alien #) A _____
☐ An alien authorized to work until _____
(Alien # or Admission #)

Employee's Signature	Date (month/day/year)

Preparer and/or Translator Certification. *(To be completed and signed if Section 1 is prepared by a person other than the employee.) I attest, under penalty of perjury, that I have assisted in the completion of this form and that to the best of my knowledge the information is true and correct.*

Preparer's/Translator's Signature	Print Name

Address (Street Name and Number, City, State, Zip Code)	Date (month/day/year)

Section 2. Employer Review and Verification. To be completed and signed by employer. Examine one document from List A OR examine one document from List B and one from List C, as listed on the reverse of this form, and record the title, number and expiration date, if any, of the document(s).

List A	OR	List B	AND	List C
Document title:				
Issuing authority:				
Document #:				
Expiration Date (if any):				
Document #:				
Expiration Date (if any):				

CERTIFICATION - I attest, under penalty of perjury, that I have examined the document(s) presented by the above-named employee, that the above-listed document(s) appear to be genuine and to relate to the employee named, that the employee began employment on *(month/day/year)* _____ and that to the best of my knowledge the employee is eligible to work in the United States. (State employment agencies may omit the date the employee began employment.)

Signature of Employer or Authorized Representative	Print Name	Title

Business or Organization Name	Address (Street Name and Number, City, State, Zip Code)	Date (month/day/year)

Section 3. Updating and Reverification. To be completed and signed by employer.

A. New Name (if applicable)	B. Date of Rehire (month/day/year) (if applicable)

C. If employee's previous grant of work authorization has expired, provide the information below for the document that establishes current employment eligibility.

Document Title: _____ Document #: _____ Expiration Date (if any): _____

I attest, under penalty of perjury, that to the best of my knowledge, this employee is eligible to work in the United States, and if the employee presented document(s), the document(s) I have examined appear to be genuine and to relate to the individual.

Signature of Employer or Authorized Representative	Date (month/day/year)

NOTE: This is the 1991 edition of the Form I-9 that has been rebranded with a current printing date to reflect the recent transition from the INS to DHS and its components.

Form I-9 (Rev. 05/31/05)Y Page 2

LISTS OF ACCEPTABLE DOCUMENTS

LIST A		LIST B		LIST C
Documents that Establish Both Identity and Employment Eligibility	**OR**	**Documents that Establish Identity**	**AND**	**Documents that Establish Employment Eligibility**

LIST A — Documents that Establish Both Identity and Employment Eligibility

1. U.S. Passport (unexpired or expired)

2. Certificate of U.S. Citizenship (Form N-560 or N-561)

3. Certificate of Naturalization (Form N-550 or N-570)

4. Unexpired foreign passport, with I-551 stamp or attached Form I-94 indicating unexpired employment authorization

5. Permanent Resident Card or Alien Registration Receipt Card with photograph (Form I-151 or I-551)

6. Unexpired Temporary Resident Card (Form I-688)

7. Unexpired Employment Authorization Card (Form I-688A)

8. Unexpired Reentry Permit (Form I-327)

9. Unexpired Refugee Travel Document (Form 1-571)

10. Unexpired Employment Authorization Document issued by DHS that contains a photograph (Form I-688B)

LIST B — Documents that Establish Identity

1. Driver's license or ID card issued by a state or outlying possession of the United States provided it contains a photograph or information such as name, date of birth, gender, height, eye color and address

2. ID card issued by federal, state or local government agencies or entities, provided it contains a photograph or information such as name, date of birth, gender, height, eye color and address

3. School ID card with a photograph

4.†† Voter's registration card

5.†† U.S. Military card or draft record

6.† Military dependent's ID card

7. U.S. Coast Guard Merchant Mariner Card

8.†† Native American tribal document

9. Driver's license issued by a Canadian government authority

For persons under age 18 who are unable to present a document listed above:

10. School record or report card

11. Clinic, doctor or hospital record

12. Day-care or nursery school record

LIST C — Documents that Establish Employment Eligibility

1. U.S. social security card issued by the Social Security Administration (other than a card stating it is not valid for employment)

2. Certification of Birth Abroad issued by the Department of State (Form FS-545 or Form DS-1350)

3. Original or certified copy of a birth certificate issued by a state, county, municipal authority or outlying possession of the United States bearing an official seal

4.†† Native American tribal document

5. † U.S. Citizen ID Card (Form I-197)

6. ID Card for use of Resident Citizen in the United States (Form I-179)

7. Unexpired employment authorization document issued by DHS (other than those listed under List A)

Illustrations of many of these documents appear in Part 8 of the Handbook for Employers (M-274)

Form I-9 (Rev. 05/31/05)Y Page 3

APPENDIX 21:
LIST OF ACCEPTABLE EMPLOYEE IDENTIFICATION DOCUMENTS

The following is a partial list of valid documents from which the employee may choose to present proof of identity to his or her employer in conjunction with the completion of Form I-9. The employee may choose one document from LIST A. Or, the employee may choose two documents, one from LIST B that shows identity and one from LIST C that shows work authorization.

LIST A—DOCUMENTS THAT ESTABLISH BOTH IDENTITY AND EMPLOYMENT ELIGIBILITY

1. U.S. Passport (unexpired or expired)

2. Certificate of U.S. Citizenship (INS Form N-560 or N-561)

3. Certificate of Naturalization (INS Form N-550 or N-570)

4. Unexpired Foreign Passport (with I-551 stamp or attached Form I-94 indicating unexpired employment authorization)

5. Permanent Resident Card or Alien Registration Receipt Card with Photograph (Form I-151 or I-551)

6. Unexpired Temporary Resident Card (Form I-688)

7. Unexpired Employment Authorization Card (Form I-688A)

8. Unexpired Reentry Permit (Form I-327)

9. Unexpired Refugee Travel Document (Form I 571)

10. Unexpired Employment Authorization Document Issued by DHS with Photograph (Form I-688B)

LIST B—DOCUMENTS THAT ESTABLISH IDENTITY

1. Driver's License or ID Card Issued by a State or Outlying Possession of the United States (provided it contains a photograph or information such as name, date of birth, gender, height, eye color and address)

2. ID Card Issued by Federal, State or Local Government Agencies or Entities (provided it contains a photograph or information such as name, date of birth, gender, height, eye color and address)

3. School ID Card with Photograph

4. Voter's Registration Card

5. U.S. Military Card or Draft Record

6. Military Dependent's ID Card

7. U.S. Coast Guard Merchant Mariner Card

8. Native American Tribal Document

9. Driver's License Issued by a Canadian Government Authority

FOR PERSONS UNDER AGE 18 WHO ARE UNABLE TO PRESENT A DOCUMENT LISTED ABOVE:

10. School Record or Report Card

11. Clinic, Doctor or Hospital Record

12. Day Care or Nursery School Record

LIST C—DOCUMENTS THAT ESTABLISH EMPLOYMENT ELIGIBILITY

1. U.S. Social Security Card Issued by the Social Security Administration (other than a card stating it is not valid for employment)

2. Certification of Birth Abroad Issued by the Department of State (Form FS-545 or Form DS-1350)

3. Original or Certified Copy of a Birth Certificate Issued by a State, County, Municipal Authority or Outlying Possession of the United States Bearing an Official Seal

4. Native American Tribal Document

5. U.S. Citizen ID Card (Form I-197)

6. ID Card for Use of Resident Citizen in the United States (Form I-179)

7. Unexpired Employment Authorization Document Issued by DHS (other than those listed under List A)

APPENDIX 22:
TABLE OF STATE MINIMUM WAGE LAWS
(AS OF APRIL 2006)

STATE	BASIC MINIMUM HOURLY RATE
ALABAMA	No State Minimum Wage Law
ALASKA	$7.15
ARIZONA	No State Minimum Wage Law
ARKANSAS	$5.15 (applicable to employers of 4 or more employees; state law excludes from coverage any employment that is subject to the Federal Fair Labor Standards Act)
CALIFORNIA	$6.75
COLORADO	$5.15
CONNECTICUT	$7.40 (increasing to $7.65 on 1/1/07)
DELAWARE	$6.15 (state minimum wage automatically replaced with the Federal minimum wage rate if it is higher than the State minimum)
DISTRICT OF COLUMBIA	$7.00 (automatically set at $1.00 above Federal minimum wage rate)
FLORIDA	$6.40
GEORGIA	$5.15 (applicable to employers of 6 or more employees; state law excludes from coverage any employment that is subject to the Federal Fair Labor Standards Act when the Federal rate is greater than the State rate)
HAWAII	$6.75 (increasing to $7.25 on 1/1/07; state law excludes from coverage any employment that is subject to the Federal Fair Labor Standards Act unless the State wage rate is higher than the Federal)
IDAHO	$5.15

STATE	BASIC MINIMUM HOURLY RATE
ILLINOIS	$6.50 (applicable to employers of 4 or more employees excluding family members)
INDIANA	$5.15 (applicable to employers of 2 or more employees; state law excludes from coverage any employment that is subject to the Federal Fair Labor Standards Act)
IOWA	$5.15 (state minimum wage automatically replaced with the Federal minimum wage rate if it is higher than the State minimum)
KANSAS	$2.65 (state law excludes from coverage any employment that is subject to the Federal Fair Labor Standards Act)
KENTUCKY	$5.15 (state adopts the Federal minimum wage rate by reference)
LOUISIANA	No State Minimum Wage Law
MAINE	$6.50 (state minimum wage automatically replaced with the Federal minimum wage rate if it is higher than the State minimum)
MARYLAND	$6.15
MASSACHUSETTS	$6.75 (automatically increases to 10 cents above the rate set in the Fair Labor Standards Act if the Federal minimum wage equals or becomes higher than the State minimum)
MICHIGAN	$5.15 (applicable to employers of 2 or more employees; state law excludes from coverage any employment that is subject to the Federal Fair Labor Standards Act unless the State wage rate is higher than the Federal)
MINNESOTA	$6.15 (applies to large employers with annual receipts of $625,000 or more); $5.25 (applies to smaller employers with annual receipts of less than $625,000)
MISSISSIPPI	No State Minimum Wage Law
MISSOURI	$5.15 (state law excludes from coverage any employment that is subject to the Federal Fair Labor Standards Act)
MONTANA	$5.15 (state adopts the Federal minimum wage rate by reference; lesser rate of $4.00 per hour applies to businesses with gross annual sales of $110,000 or less)
NEBRASKA	$5.15 (applicable to employers of 4 or more employees)
NEVADA	$5.15 (state adopts the Federal minimum wage rate by reference)

STATE	BASIC MINIMUM HOURLY RATE
NEW HAMPSHIRE	$5.15 (minimum wage is automatically replaced with the Federal minimum wage rate if it is higher)
NEW JERSEY	$6.15 (increasing to $7.15 on 10/1/06; state minimum wage law adopts the Federal minimum wage rate by reference)
NEW MEXICO	$5.15
NEW YORK	$6.75 (increasing to $7.15 on 1/1/07; minimum wage is automatically replaced with the Federal minimum wage rate if it is higher)
NORTH CAROLINA	$5.15 (state law excludes from coverage any employment that is subject to the Federal Fair Labor Standards Act; state adopts the Federal minimum wage rate by reference)
NORTH DAKOTA	$5.15
OHIO	$5.15
OKLAHOMA	$5.15 (state adopts the Federal minimum wage rate by reference; applies to employers of 10 or more full-time employees at any one location, and employers with annual gross sales over $100,000 irrespective of number of full-time employees; lesser rate of $2.00 applies to all other employers)
OREGON	$7.50
PENNSYLVANIA	$5.15 (state adopts the Federal minimum wage rate by reference)
RHODE ISLAND	$7.10
SOUTH CAROLINA	No State Minimum Wage Law
SOUTH DAKOTA	$5.15
TENNESSEE	No State Minimum Wage Law
TEXAS	$5.15 (state adopts the Federal minimum wage rate by reference)
UTAH	$5.15 (state law excludes from coverage any employment that is subject to the Federal Fair Labor Standards Act; state law authorizes the adoption of the Federal minimum rate via administrative action)
VERMONT	$7.25 (applicable to employers of 2 or more employees; minimum wage is automatically replaced with the Federal minimum wage rate if it is higher than the State minimum)
VIRGINIA	$5.15 (applicable to employers of 4 or more employees; state adopts the Federal minimum wage rate by reference)

STATE	BASIC MINIMUM HOURLY RATE
WASHINGTON	$7.63
WEST VIRGINIA	$5.15 (applies to employers of 6 or more employees in one location; state law excludes from coverage any employment that is subject to the Federal Fair Labor Standards Act)
WISCONSIN	$5.70
WYOMING	$5.15

Source: U.S. Department of Labor, Employment Standards Administration, Wage and Hour Division.

APPENDIX 23:
DIRECTORY OF STATE DEPARTMENTS OF LABOR

STATE	ADDRESS	TELEPHONE	FAX	INTERNET ADDRESS
ALABAMA	Department of Labor P.O. Box 303500 Montgomery, AL 36130-3500	334-242-3460	334-240-3417	www.dir.state.al.us
ALASKA	Department of Labor P.O. Box 21149 Juneau, AK 99802-1149	907-465-2700	907-465-2784	www.labor.state.ak.us
ARIZONA	State Labor Department P.O. Box 19070 Phoenix, AZ 85005-9070	602-542-4411	602-542-3104	www.ica.state.az.us
ARKANSAS	Department of Labor 10421 West Markham Little Rock, AR 72205	501-682-4541	501-682-4535	www.state.ar.us/labor

STATE	ADDRESS	TELEPHONE	FAX	INTERNET ADDRESS
CALIFORNIA	Department of Industrial Relations 455 Golden Gate Ave. 10th Floor San Francisco, CA 94102	415-703-5050	415-703-5059	www.dir.ca.gov
COLORADO	Department of Labor and Employment 2 Park Central, Suite 400 Denver, CO 80202-2117	303-620-4701	303-620-4714	http://cdle.state.co.us
CONNECTICUT	Labor Department 200 Folly Brook Boulevard Wethersfield, CT 06109-1114	860-263-6505	860-263-6529	www.ctdol.state.ct.us
DELAWARE	Department of Labor 4425 N. Market Street 4th Floor. Wilmington, DE 19802	302-761-8000	302-761-6621	www.delawareworks.com
DISTRICT OF COLUMBIA	Department of Employment Services Employment Security Building 500 "C" Street NW, Suite 600 Washington, D.C. 20001	202-724-7100	202-724-5683	does.ci.washington.dc.us
FLORIDA	Department of Labor and Employment Security 2012 Capitol Circle S.E. Hartman Building, Suite 303 Tallahassee, FL 32399-2152	850-922-7021	904-488-8930	www.state.fl.us/dles

STATE	ADDRESS	TELEPHONE	FAX	INTERNET ADDRESS
GEORGIA	Department of Labor Sussex Place - Room 600 148 International Blvd. N.E. Atlanta, GA 30303	404-656-3011	404-656-2683	www.dol.state.ga.us
HAWAII	Department of Labor and Industrial Relations 830 Punchbowl Street Room 321 Honolulu, HI 96813	808-586-8844	808-586-9099	www.dlir.state.hi.us
IDAHO	Department of Labor 317 W. Main Street Boise, ID 83735-0001	208-334-6110	208-334-6430	www.labor.state.id.us
ILLINOIS	Department of Labor 160 N. LaSalle Street 13th Floor, Suite C-1300 Chicago, IL 60601	312-793-1808	312-793-5257	www.state.il.us/agency/idol
INDIANA	Department of Labor 402 West Washington Street Room W195 Indianapolis, IN 46204-2739	317-232-2378	317-233-5381	www.state.in.us/labor
IOWA	Iowa Workforce Development 1000 East Grand Avenue Des Moines, IA 50319-0209	515-281-5365	515-281-4698	www.state.ia.us/iwd

STATE	ADDRESS	TELEPHONE	FAX	INTERNET ADDRESS
KANSAS	Department of Human Resources 401 S.W. Topeka Boulevard Topeka, KS 66603	785-296-7474	785-368-6294	www.hr.state.ks.us
KENTUCKY	Kentucky Labor Cabinet 1047 U.S. Hwy. 127 South Suite 4 Frankfort, KY 40601	502-564-3070	502-564-5387	www.state.ky.us/agencies/labor/labrhome.htm
LOUISIANA	Department of Labor P.O. Box 94094 Baton Rouge, LA 70804-9094	225-342-3011	225-342-3778	www.ldol.state.la.us
MAINE	Department of Labor 20 Union Street P.O. Box 259 Augusta, ME 04332-0259	207-287-3788	207-287-5292	janus.state.me.us/labor
MARYLAND	Department of Labor 500 N. Calvert Street Suite 401 Baltimore, MD 21202	410-230-6020	410-333-0853	www.dllr.state.md.us
MASSACHUSETTS	Department of Labor & Work Force Development 1 Ashburton Place, Rm. 2112 Boston, MA 02108	617-727-6573	617-727-1090	www.detma.org

STATE	ADDRESS	TELEPHONE	FAX	INTERNET ADDRESS
MICHIGAN	Department of Consumer & Industry Services P.O. Box 30004 Lansing, MI 48909	517-373-3034	517-373-2129	www.cis.state.mi.us
MINNESOTA	Department of Labor and Industry 443 Lafayette Road St. Paul, MN 55155	651-296-2342	651-282-5405	www.doli.state.mn.us
MISSISSIPPI	Employment Security Commission P.O. Box 1699 Jackson, MS 39215-1699	601-961-7400	601-961-7406	www.mesc.state.ms.us
MISSOURI	Labor and Industrial Relations Commission 3315 W. Truman Boulevard Jefferson City, MO 65102	573-751-2461	573-751-7806	www.solir.state.mo.us
MONTANA	Department of Labor and Industry P.O. Box 1728 Helena, MT 59624-1728	406-444-9091	406-444-1394	http://dli.state.mt.us
NEBRASKA	Department of Labor 550 South 16th Street Lincoln, NE 68509-4600	402-471-9792	402-471-2318	www.dol.state.ne.us

STATE	ADDRESS	TELEPHONE	FAX	INTERNET ADDRESS
NEVADA	Business and Industry 555 E. Washington Avenue Suite 4100 Las Vegas, NV 89101	702-486-2650	702-486-2660	www.state.nv.us/labor
NEW HAMPSHIRE	Department of Labor 95 Pleasant Street Concord, NH 03301	603-271-3171	603-271-6852	www.state.nh.us/dol
NEW JERSEY	New Jersey Dept. of Labor John Fitch Plaza 13th Floor, Suite D Trenton, NJ 08625-0110	609-292-2323	609-633-9271	www.state.nj.us/labor
NEW MEXICO	Department of Labor 401 Broadway N.E. Albuquerque, NM 87103-1928	505-841-8408	505-841-8491	www.state.nm.us/dol
NEW YORK	Department of Labor State Campus, Building 12 Albany, NY 12240	518-457-2741	518-457-6908	www.labor.state.ny.us
NORTH CAROLINA	Department of Labor 4 West Edenton Street Raleigh, NC 27601-1092	919-733-0360	919-733-6197	www.dol.state.nc.us
NORTH DAKOTA	Department of Labor State Capitol Building 600 East Boulevard, Dept. 406 Bismarck, ND 58505-0340	701-328-2660	701-328-2031	www.state.nd.us/labor

STATE	ADDRESS	TELEPHONE	FAX	INTERNET ADDRESS
OHIO	Department of Commerce 77 South High St., 23rd Floor Columbus, OH 43266	614-466-7053	614-466-5650	http://www.state.oh.us/ohio/agency .htm
OKLAHOMA	Department of Labor 4001 N. Lincoln Blvd. Oklahoma City, OK 73105-5212	405-528-1500	405-528-5751	www.state.ok.us/~okdol
OREGON	Bureau of Labor and Industries 800 NE Oregon Street #32 Portland, OR 97232	503-731-4070	503-7314103	www.boli.state.or.us
PENNSYLVANIA	Department of Labor and Industry 1700 Labor and Industry Building 7th and Forster Streets Harrisburg, PA 17120	717-787-3756	717-787-8826	www.li.state.pa.us
RHODE ISLAND	Department of Labor and Training 1511 Pontiac Avenue Cranston, RI 02920	401-462-8870	401-462-8872	www.det.state.ri.us
SOUTH CAROLINA	Department of Labor Synergy Center - King St. Building 110 Center View Drive Columbia, SC 29211-1329	803-896-4300	803-896-4393	www.llr.state.sc.us

STATE	ADDRESS	TELEPHONE	FAX	INTERNET ADDRESS
SOUTH DAKOTA	Department of Labor 700 Governors Drive Pierre, SD 57501-2291	605-773-3101	605-773-4211	www.state.sd.us/dol/dol.htm
TENNESSEE	Department of Labor 710 James Robertson Pky. 8th Floor Nashville, TN 37243-0655	615-741-6642	615-741-5078	www.state.tn.us
TEXAS	Texas Workforce Commission 101 East 15th Street Rm 618 Austin, TX 78778	512-463-0735	512-475-2321	www.twc.state.tx.us
UTAH	Utah Labor Commission P.O. Box 146600 Salt Lake City, UT 84111-2316	801-530-6880	801-530-6390	www.labor.state.ut.us
VERMONT	Department of Labor & Industry National Life Building Drawer #20 Montpelier, VT 05620-3401	802-828-2288	802-828-0408	www.state.vt.us/labind
VIRGINIA	Dept. of Labor and Industry Powers-Taylor Building 13 S. 13th Richmond, VA 23219	804-786-2377	804-371-6524	www.dli.state.va.us

STATE	ADDRESS	TELEPHONE	FAX	INTERNET ADDRESS
WASHINGTON	Department of Labor & Industries P.O. Box 44001 Olympia, WA 98504-4001	360-902-4213	360-902-4202	www.wa.gov/lni
WEST VIRGINIA	Division of Labor State Capitol Complex Building #3 Room 319 Charleston, WV 25305	304-558-7890	304-558-3797	www.state.wv.us/labor
WISCONSIN	Department of Workforce Development 201 East Washington Avenue Suite #400 Madison, WI 53707-7946	608-266-7552	608-266-1784	www.dwd.state.wi.us
WYOMING	Department of Employment Herschler Building, 2-East 122 W. 25th Street Cheyenne, WY 82002	307-777-7672	307-777-5805	http://wydoe.state.wy.us/labstd

APPENDIX 24:
INDEPENDENT CONTRACTOR AGREEMENT

This Agreement dated [Date], is by and between [Company Name and Address] (Company), and [Independent Contractor Name and Address] (Contractor).

For valuable consideration, Company and Contractor agree as follows:

ARTICLE ONE: SERVICES

1. Contractor agrees to perform the following services for Company: [Specify]

ARTICLE TWO: COMPLETION

2. Contractor agrees that the services described in Article One will be commenced on [Start Date], and will be completed by [End Date].

ARTICLE THREE: LABOR

3. Contractor agrees to hire and compensate Contractor's own employees to perform services under this contract.

ARTICLE FOUR: MATERIALS

4. Contractor agrees to furnish all materials necessary to perform services under this contract.

ARTICLE FIVE: PAYMENT

5. Company agrees to pay Contractor the total amount of [Dollar Amount] for Contractor's services under this contract. Such payment shall be made as follows: [Specify]

ARTICLE SIX: MISCELLANEOUS PROVISIONS

6. The parties agree that Contractor is not an employee of Company and Contractor shall not represent that he or she is an employee of the Company.

7. Contractor agrees to indemnify and hold Company harmless from any claims or liabilities arising out of the performance of Contractor's services under this contract.

8. This Agreement contains the entire understanding of the parties.

9. Any modification of this agreement must be in writing and signed by both parties.

10. This Agreement is being made in [State Name] and shall be construed and enforced according to the laws of that state.

11. Additional Terms: [Specify]

IN WITNESS WHEREOF, the parties have duly executed this Agreement as of the date first written above.

_____

Company

_____

Independent Contractor

APPENDIX 25:
EMPLOYEE/INDEPENDENT CONTRACTOR FACTORS

FACTOR	EMPLOYEE	INDEPENDENT CONTRACTOR
INSTRUCTIONS	Employees comply with instructions about when, where, and how work is to be performed.	Contractors set their own hours and do the job in their own way.
TRAINING	Employees are trained to perform services in a particular way. They are required to take correspondence courses and attend meetings. Other methods also indicate the employer wants the services performed in a particular way.	Contractors use their own methods and receive no training from the purchaser of their services.
INTEGRATION	Services of an employee are merged into the business. Success and continuation of the business depends upon these services. The employer coordinates work with that of others.	The success and continuation of the business aren't dependent on services provided by a contractor.
SERVICES RENDERED PERSONALLY	Services must be rendered personally. An employee does not engage other people to do the work.	Contractors are able to assign their own workers to do the job.

FACTOR	EMPLOYEE	INDEPENDENT CONTRACTOR
HIRING/SUPERVISING/PAYING	An employee hires, supervises and pays workers at the direction of the employer (i.e., acts as foreman or representative of the employer).	Contractors hire, supervise and pay the other workers as the result of a contract. A contractor agrees to provide materials and labor and is responsible for the results.
CONTINUING RELATIONSHIP	An employee continues to work for the same person year after year.	Contractors are hired to do one job. There is no continuous relationship.
SET HOURS OF WORK	An employee's hours and days are set by the employer.	Contractors are masters of their own time.
FULL TIME REQUIRED	An employee normally works full time for an employer.	Contractors are free to work when and for whom they choose.
DOING WORK ON EMPLOYER'S PREMISES	Employees work on the premises of an employer; or on a route, or at a site, designated by the employer.	Contractors work off an employer's premises and use their own offices, desks, and telephones.
ORDER OR SEQUENCE SET	An employee performs services in the order or sequence set by the employer. Salespersons report to the office at specified times, follow-up on leads, and perform certain tasks at certain times.	Services are performed at a contractor's own pace. Salespersons work their own schedules and usually have their own offices.
ORAL OR WRITTEN REPORTS	Employees are required to submit regular oral or written reports to the employer.	Contractors submit no reports.
PAYMENT BY HOUR/WEEK/MONTH	Employees are paid by the employer in regular amounts at stated intervals.	A contractor is paid by the job on a straight commission.
PAYMENT OF BUSINESS AND/OR TRAVEL EXPENSES	The employer pays employees' business and/or travel expenses.	Contractors take care of their own expenses and are accountable only to themselves for expenses.

FACTOR	EMPLOYEE	INDEPENDENT CONTRACTOR
FURNISHING OF TOOLS/MATERIALS	An employer furnishes tools, materials, etc.	Contractors furnish their own tools, etc.
SIGNIFICANT INVESTMENT	An employee has no significant investment in the facilities used to perform services.	A contractor has a real, essential and significant investment.
REALIZATION OF PROFIT OR LOSS	An employee cannot realize a profit or loss by making good or bad decisions.	Contractors can realize a profit or suffer a loss as a result of their services or decisions.
WORKING FOR MORE THAN ONE FIRM AT A TIME	An employee usually works for one employee at a time.	An independent contractor works for a number of persons or firms at the same time.
MAKING SERVICES AVAILABLE TO THE GENERAL PUBLIC	An employee does not make services available to the general public.	Contractors have their own offices and assistants. They hold business licenses, are listed in business directories, maintain business telephones, and otherwise generally make their services available to the public.
RIGHT TO FIRE	An employee can be discharged at any time.	Contractors cannot be fired so long as product results meet contract specifications.
RIGHT TO QUIT	Employees can quit their jobs at any time without incurring liability.	Contractors agree to complete a specific job and are responsible for satisfactory completion; or they are legally obligated to make good for any failure.

SOURCE: Internal Revenue Service

APPENDIX 26:
DIRECTORY OF OCCUPATIONAL SAFETY
AND HEALTH ADMINISTRATION OFFICES

STATE	ADDRESS	TELEPHONE NUMBER	FAX NUMBER
Alabama	432 Martha Parham West P.O. Box 870388 Tuscaloosa, AL 35487	205-348-7138	205-348-3049
Alaska	3301 Eagle Street P.O. Box 107022 Anchorage, AL 99510	907-269-4954	907-269-4950
Arizona	800 West Washington Phoenix, AZ 85007	602-542-5795	602-542-1614
Arkansas	10421 West Markham Little Rock, AR 72205	501-682-4522	501-682-4532
California	455 Golden Gate Avenue Room 5246 San Francisco, CA 94102	415-703-4441	415-972-8513
Colorado	110 Veterinary Science Building Fort Collins, CO 80523	303-491-6151	303-491-7778
Connecticut	200 Folly Brook Boulevard Wethersfield, CT 06109	203-566-4550	203-566-6916
Delaware	4425 Market Street Wilmington, DE 19802	302-761-8219	302-761-6601
District of Columbia	950 Upshur Street N.W. Washington, DC 20011	202-576-6339	202-576-7282
Florida	2002 St. Augustine Road Building E, Suite 45 Tallahassee, FL 32399	904-488-3044	904-922-4538

STATE	ADDRESS	TELEPHONE NUMBER	FAX NUMBER
Georgia	Georgia Institute of Technology O'Keefe Building Room 22 Atlanta, GA 30332	404-894-2646	404-894-8275
Hawaii	830 Punchbowl Street Honolulu, HI 96813	808-586-9100	808-586-9099
Idaho	1910 University Drive Boise, ID 83725	208-385-3283	208-385-4411
Illinois	State of Illinois Center 100 West Randolph Street Suite 3-400 Chicago, IL 60601	312-814-2337	312-814-7238
Indiana	402 West Washington Indianapolis, IN 46204	317-232-2688	317-2320748
Iowa	1000 East Grand Avenue Des Moines, IA 50319	515-281-5352	515-281-4831
Kansas	512 South West 6th Street Topeka, KS 66603	913-296-7476	913-206-1775
Kentucky	1049 U.S. Highway 127 South Frankfort, KY 40601	502-564-6895	502-564-4769
Louisiana	P.O. Box 94094 Baton Rouge, LA 70804	504-342-9601	504-342-5158
Maine	State House Station #82 Augusta, ME 04333	207-624-6460	207-624-6449
Maryland	501 St. Paul Place 3rd Floor Baltimore, MD 21202	410-333-4210	410-333-8308
Massachusetts	1001 Watertown Street West Newton, MA 02165	617-969-7177	617-969-4581
Michigan	3423 North Martin Luther King Boulevard Lansing, MI 48909	517-335-8250	517-335-8010
Minnesota	443 Lafayette Road Saint Paul, MN 55155	612-297-2393	612-297-1953
Mississippi	2906 North State Street Suite 201 Jackson, MS 39216	601-987-3981	601-987-3890
Missouri	3315 West Truman Boulevard Jefferson City, MO 65109	573-751-3403	573-751-3721

STATE	ADDRESS	TELEPHONE NUMBER	FAX NUMBER
Montana	P.O. Box 1728 Helena, MT 59624	406-444-6418	406-444-4140
Nebraska	State Office Building 301 Centennial Mall South Lower Level Lincoln, NE 68509	402-471-4717	402-471-5039
Nevada	2500 West Washington Las Vegas, NV 89106	702486-5016	702-486-5331
New Hampshire	6 Hazen Drive Concord, NH 03301	603-271-2024	603-271-2667
New Jersey	Station Plaza 4 CN953 22 South Clinton Avenue Trenton, NJ 08625	609-292-2424	609-292-4409
New Mexico	525 Camino de Los Marquez Suite 3 P.O. Box 26110 Santa Fe, NM 87502	505-827-4230	505-827-4422
New York	State Office Campus Building 12 Room 457 Albany, NY 12240	518-457-2481	518-457-5545
North Carolina	319 Chapanoke Road Suite 105 Raleigh, NC 27603	919-662-4644	919-662-4671
North Dakota	1200 Missouri Avenue Room 304 Bismarck, ND 58506	701-328-5188	701-328-5200
Ohio	145 S. Front Street Columbus, OH 43216	614-644-2246	614-644-3133
Oklahoma	4001 North Lincoln Boulevard Oklahoma City, OK 73105	405-528-1500	405-528-5751
Oregon	350 Winter Street NE Room 430 Salem, OR 97310	503-378-3272	503-378-5729
Pennsylvania	Indiana University of Pennsylvania Safety Sciences Department 205 Uhler Hall Indiana, PA 15705	412-357-2561	412-357-2385

STATE	ADDRESS	TELEPHONE NUMBER	FAX NUMBER
Rhode Island	3 Capital Hill Providence, RI 02908	401-277-2438	401-277-6953
South Carolina	3600 Forest Drive P.O. Box 11329 Columbia, SC 29211	803-734-9614	803-734-9741
South Dakota	South Dakota State University, West Hall Box 510 907 Harvey Dunn Street Brookings, SD 57007	605-688-4101	605-688-6290
Tennessee	710 James Robertson Parkway 3rd Floor Nashville, TN 37243	615-741-7036	615-741-3325
Texas	4000 South I H 35 Austin, TX 78704	512-440-3834	512-440-3831
Utah	160 East 300 South Salt Lake City, UT 84114	801-530-6868	801-530-6992
Vermont	National Life Building Drawer 20 Montpelier, VT 05602	802-828-2765	802-828-2748
Virginia	13 South 13th Street Richmond, VA 23219	804-786-6539	804-786-8418
Washington	P.O. Box 44643 Olympia, WA 98504	360-902-5638	360-902-5459
West Virginia	Capitol Complex Building #3 1800 East Washington Street Room 319 Charleston, WV 25305	304-558-7890	304-558-3797
Wisconsin	1414 East Washington Avenue Madison, WI 53703	608-266-8579	608-266-9711
Wyoming	Herschler Building 2 East 122 West 25th Street Cheyenne, WY 82008	307-777-7786	307-777-3646

APPENDIX 27:
DIRECTORY OF STATE WORKERS'
COMPENSATION BOARDS

STATE	ADDRESS	TELEPHONE
ALABAMA	Workers' Compensation Division Department of Industrial Relations Industrial Relations Building Montgomery, AL 36131	334-242-2868
ALASKA	Workers' Compensation Division Department of Labor 1111 West 8th Street, Suite 307 P.O. Box 25512 Juneau, AK 99802-5512	907-465-2790
ARIZONA	Industrial Commission 800 West Washington Street P. O. Box 19070 Phoenix, AZ 85005-9070	602-542-4411
ARKANSAS	Workers' Compensation Commission 4th and Spring Streets P. O. Box 950 Little Rock, AR 72203-9050	501-682-3930
CALIFORNIA	Division of Workers' Compensation 45 Fremont Street Suite 3160 P. O. Box 420603 San Francisco, CA 94142	415-975-0700
COLORADO	Division of Workers' Compensation 1515 Arapahoe Street Denver, CO 80202	303-575-8700
CONNECTICUT	Workers' Compensation Commission 21 Oak Street Hartford, CT 06106	860-493-1500
DELAWARE	Industrial Accident Board 4425 N. Market Street, 3rd Floor Wilmington, DE 19802	302-761-8200

STATE	ADDRESS	TELEPHONE
DISTRICT OF COLUMBIA	Office of Workers' Compensation 1200 Upshur St. NW, 2nd Floor Washington, DC 20011	202-576-6265
FLORIDA	Division of Workers' Compensation 301 Forrest Building 2728 Centerview Drive Tallahassee, FL 32399-0680	904-488-2514
GEORGIA	Board of Workers' Compensation 270 Peachtree Street NW Atlanta, GA 30303-1205	404-656-3875
HAWAII	Disability Compensation Division Department of Labor and Industrial Relations 830 Punchbowl Street, Room 211 P. O. Box 3769 Honolulu, HI 96812	808-586-9151
IDAHO	Industrial Commission Statehouse Mail, 317 Main Street P. O. Box 83720 Boise, ID 83720-0041	208-334-6000
ILLINOIS	Industrial Commission 100 West Randolph Street Suite 8-200 Chicago, IL 60601	312-814-6500
INDIANA	Workers' Compensation Board Room W-196 402 West Washington Street Indianapolis, IN 46204	317-232-3808
IOWA	Division of Industrial Services Iowa Workforce Development 1000 East Grand Avenue Des Moines, IA 50319	515-281-5934
KANSAS	Division of Workers' Compensation Department of Human Resources 800 SW Jackson Street, Suite 600 Topeka, KS 66612-1227	913-296-3441
KENTUCKY	Department of Workers Claims 1270 Louisville Road Perimeter Park West, Bldg. C Frankfort, KY 40601	502-564-5550
LOUISIANA	Office of Workers' Compensation 1001 North 23rd Street P. O. Box 94040 Baton Rouge, LA 70802-9040	504-342-7555

STATE	ADDRESS	TELEPHONE
MAINE	Workers' Compensation Board 27 State House Station Augusta, ME 04333	207-287-3751
MARYLAND	Workers' Compensation Commission 6 North Liberty Street Baltimore, MD 21201-3785	410-767-0900
MASSACHUSETTS	Dept. of Industrial Accidents 600 Washington Street, 7th Floor Boston, MA 02111	617-727-4900
MICHIGAN	Bureau of Workers' Disability Compensation 201 North Washington Square P. O. Box 30016 Lansing, MI 48909	517-322-1296
MINNESOTA	Division of Workers' Compensation Department of Labor and Industry 443 Lafayette Road North St. Paul, MN 55155-4319	612-296-6490
MISSISSIPPI	Workers' Compensation Commission 1428 Lakeland Drive P. O. Box 5300 Jackson, MS 39296-5300	601-987-4200
MISSOURI	Division of Workers' Compensation Department of Labor and Industrial Relations P. O. Box 58 Jefferson City, MO 65102	573-751-4231
MONTANA	Employment Relations Division Department of Labor and Industry 1805 Prospect Avenue P. O. Box 8011 Helena, MT 59604-8011	406-444-6530
NEBRASKA	Workers' Compensation Court Capitol Building P. O. Box 98908 Lincoln, NE 68509-8908	402-471-2568
NEVADA	State Industrial Insurance System 515 East Musser Street Carson City, NV 89714	702-687-5220
NEW HAMPSHIRE	Workers' Compensation Division Department of Labor 95 Pleasant Street Concord, NH 03301	603-271-3176
NEW JERSEY	Division of Workers' Compensation Department of Labor, C. N. 381 Trenton, NJ 08625-0381	609-292-2414

STATE	ADDRESS	TELEPHONE
NEW MEXICO	Workers' Compensation Admin. 2410 Centre Drive SE P. O. Box 27198 Albuquerque, NM 87125-7198	505-841-6000
NEW YORK	Workers' Compensation Board 100 Broadway-Menands Albany, NY 12241	518-474-6670
NORTH CAROLINA	Industrial Commission Dobbs Building 430 North Salisbury Street Raleigh, NC 27611	919-733-4820
NORTH DAKOTA	Workers' Compensation Bureau 500 East Front Avenue Bismarck, ND 58504-5685	701-328-3800
OHIO	Bureau of Workers' Compensation 30 West Spring Street Columbus, OH 43266-0581	614-466-8751
OKLAHOMA	Workers' Compensation Court 1915 North Stiles Avenue Oklahoma City, OK 73105-4904	405-557-7600
OREGON	Workers' Compensation Division 350 Winter Street NE Salem, OR 97310	503-945-7881
PENNSYLVANIA	Bureau of Workers' Compensation Department of Labor and Industry 1171 So. Cameron Street, Rm. 103 Harrisburg, PA 17104-2501	717-783-5421
PUERTO RICO	Industrial Commission G.P.O. Box 364466 San Juan, PR 00936-4466	809-783-2028
RHODE ISLAND	Division of Workers' Compensation Department of Labor 610 Manton Avenue P.O. Box 3500 Providence, RI 02909	401-457-1800
SOUTH CAROLINA	Workers' Compensation Commission 1612 Marion Street P. O. Box 1715 Columbia, SC 29202-1715	803-737-5700
SOUTH DAKOTA	Division of Labor & Management Department of Labor 700 Governors Dr. Kneip Bldg. Pierre, SD 57501-2291	605-773-3681

STATE	ADDRESS	TELEPHONE
TENNESSEE	Division of Workers' Compensation Department of Labor Gateway Plaza, 2nd Floor 710 James Robertson Parkway Nashville,. TN 37243-0661	615-741-2395
TEXAS	Workers' Compensation Commission Southfield Building 4000 South IH-35 Austin, TX 78704-7491	512-448-7900
UTAH	Industrial Accident Division Industrial Commission 160 East 300 South, 3rd Floor P. O. Box 146610 Salt Lake City, UT 84114 6610	801-530-6800
VERMONT	Department of Labor and Industry National Life Building Drawer 20 Montpelier, VT 05620-3401	802-828-2286
VIRGINIA	Workers' Compensation Commission 1000 DMV Drive Richmond, VA 23220	804-367-8600
VIRGIN ISLANDS	Workers' Compensation Division Department of Labor 2131 Hospital Street St. Croix, VI 00820-4666	809-692-9390
WASHINGTON	Department of Labor and Industries 7273 Linderson Way, SW Tumwater, WA 98501-4850	360-902-5800
WEST VIRGINIA	Workers' Compensation Division 4700 MacCorkle Avenue SE Charleston, WV 25304	304-926-5048
WISCONSIN	Workers' Compensation Division Department of Workforce Development 201 East Washington Avenue P. O. Box 7901 Madison, WI 53707	608-266-1340
WYOMING	Workers' Compensation Division 122 West 25th Street 2nd Floor Herschler Building, East Wing Cheyenne, WY 82002-0700	307 777 7159

APPENDIX 28:
DIRECTORY OF UNITED STATES EQUAL EMPLOYMENT OPPORTUNITY COMMISSION OFFICES

EEOC OFFICE	ADDRESS	TELEPHONE NUMBER	TTY NUMBER
Headquarters	1801 L Street N.W. Washington, D.C. 20507	202-663-4900	202-663-4494
Albuquerque District Office	505 Marquette Street N.W., Suite 900 Albuquerque, NM 87102	505-248-5201	505-248-5240
Atlanta District Office	100 Alabama Street Suite 4R30 Atlanta, GA 30303	404-562-6800	404-562-6801
Baltimore District Office	City Crescent Building 3rd Floor Baltimore, MD 21201	410-962-3932	410-962-6065
Birmingham District Office	1900 3rd Avenue North Suite 101 Birmingham, AL 35203-2397	205-731-1359	205-731-0175
Boston Area Office	1 Congress Street 10th Floor, Room 1001 Boston, MA 02114	617-565-3200	617-565-3204
Buffalo Local Office	6 Fountain Plaza Suite 350 Buffalo, NY 14202	716-846-4441	716-846-5923
Charlotte District Office	129 West Trade Street Suite 400 Charlotte, NC 28202	704-344-6682	704-344-6684
Chicago District Office	500 West Madison Street Suite 2800 Chicago, IL 60661	312-353-2713	312-353-2421

EEOC OFFICE	ADDRESS	TELEPHONE NUMBER	TTY NUMBER
Cincinnati Area Office	525 Vine Street Suite 810 Cincinnati, OH 45202-3122	513-684-2851	513-684-2074
Cleveland District Office	1660 West Second Street Suite 850 Cleveland, OH 44113-1454	216-522-2001	216-522-8441
Dallas District Office	207 S. Houston Street 3rd Floor Dallas, TX 75202-4726	214-655-3355	214-655-3363
Denver District Office	303 E. 17th Avenue Suite 510 Denver, CO 80203	303-866-1300	303-866-1950
Detroit District Office	477 Michigan Avenue Room 865 Detroit, MI 48226-9704	313-226-7636	313-226-7599
El Paso Area Office	The Commons, Building C Suite 100 4171 N. Mesa Street El Paso, TX 79902	915-534-6550	915-534-6545
Fresno Local Office	1265 West Shaw Avenue Suite 103 Fresno, CA 93711	209-487-5793	209-487-5837
Greensboro Local Office	801 Summit Avenue Greensboro, NC 27405-7813	910-333-5174	910-333-5542
Greenville Local Office	Wachovia Building Suite 530 15 South Main Street Greenville, SC 29601	803-241-4400	803-241-4403
Honolulu Local Office	300 Ala Moana Boulevard, Room 7123-A P.O. Box 50082 Honolulu, HI 96850-0051	808-541-3120	808-541-3131
Houston District Office	1919 Smith Street 7th Floor Houston, TX 77002	713-209-3320	713-209-3367
Indianapolis District Office	101 W. Ohio Street Suite 1900 Indiana, IN 46204-4203	317-226-7212	317-226-5162
Jackson Area Office	207 West Amite Street Jackson, MS 39201	601-965-4537	601-965-4915

EEOC OFFICE	ADDRESS	TELEPHONE NUMBER	TTY NUMBER
Kansas City Area Office	400 State Avenue Suite 905 Kansas City, KS 66101	913-551-5655	913-551-5657
Little Rock Area Office	425 West Capitol Avenue Suite 625 Little Rock, AR 72201	501-324-5060	501-324-5481
Los Angeles District Office	255 E. Temple 4th Floor Los Angeles, CA 90012	213-894-1000	213-894-1121
Louisville Area Office	600 Dr. Martin Luther King Jr. Place Suite 268 Louisville, KY 40202	502-582-6082	502-582-6285
Memphis District Office	1407 Union Avenue Suite 521 Memphis, TN 38104	901-544-0115	901-544-0112
Miami District Office	One Biscayne Tower 2 South Biscayne Boulevard, Suite 2700 Miami, FL 33131	305-536-4491	305-536-5721
Milwaukee District Office	310 West Wisconsin Avenue, Suite 800 Milwaukee, WI 53203-2292	414-297-1111	414-297-1115
Minneapolis Area Office	330 South Second Avenue, Suite 430 Minneapolis, MN 55401-2224	612-335-4040	612-335-4045
Nashville Area Office	50 Vantage Way Suite 202 Nashville, TN 37228	615-736-5820	615-736-5870
Newark Area Office	1 Newark Center 21st Floor Newark, NJ 07102-5233	201-645-6383	201-645-3004
New Orleans District Office	701 Loyola Avenue Suite 600 New Orleans, LA 70113-9936	504-589-2329	504-589-2958
New York District Office	201 Varick Street Room 1009 New York, NY 10014	212-741-8815	212-741-2783

EEOC OFFICE	ADDRESS	TELEPHONE NUMBER	TTY NUMBER
Norfolk Area Office	World Trade Center 101 West Main Street Suite 4300 Norfolk, VA 23510	804-441-3470	804-441-3578
Oakland Local Office	1301 Clay Street Suite 1170-N Oakland, CA 94612-5217	510-637-3230	510-637-3234
Oklahoma Area Office	210 Park Avenue Oklahoma City, OK 73102	405-231-4911	405-231-5745
Philadelphia District Office	21 South 5th Street 4th Floor Philadelphia, PA 19106	215-451-5800	215-451-5814
Phoenix District Office	3300 N. Central Avenue Phoenix, AZ 85012-1848	602-640-5000	602-640-5072
Pittsburgh Area Office	1001 Liberty Avenue Suite 300 Pittsburgh, PA 15222-4187	412-644-3444	412-644-2720
Raleigh Area Office	1309 Annapolis Drive Raleigh, NC 27608-2129	919-856-4064	919-856-4296
Richmond Area Office	3600 West Broad Street Room 229 Richmond, VA 23230	804-278-4651	804-278-4654
San Antonio District Office	5410 Fredericksburg Road, Suite 200 San Antonio, TX 78229-3555	210-229-4810	210-229-4858
San Diego Area Office	401 B Street Suite 1550 San Diego, CA 92101	619-557-7235	619-557-7232
San Francisco District Office	901 Market Street Suite 500 San Francisco, CA 94103	415-356-5100	415-356-5098
San Jose Local Office	96 North 3rd Street Suite 200 San Jose, CA 95112	408-291-7352	408-291-7374
San Juan Area Office	525 F.D. Roosevelt Avenue, Plaza Las Americas, Suite 1202 San Juan, Puerto Rico 00918-8001	787-771-1464	787-771-1484

EEOC OFFICE	ADDRESS	TELEPHONE NUMBER	TTY NUMBER
Savannah Local Office	410 Mall Boulevard Suite G Savannah, GA 31406-4821	912-652-4234	912-652-4439
Seattle District Office	Federal Office Building 909 First Avenue Suite 400 Seattle, WA 98104-1061	206-220-6883	206-220-6882
St. Louis District Office	Robert A. Young Building 1222 Spruce Street Room 8.100 St. Louis, MO 63103	314-539-7800	314-539-7803
Tampa Area Office	501 East Polk Street 10th Floor Tampa, FL 33602	813-228-2310	813-228-2003
Washington Field Office	1400 L Street N.W. Suite 200 Washington, D.C. 20005	Phone: 202-275-7377	202-275-7518

Source: U.S. Equal Employment Opportunity Commission.

APPENDIX 29:
APPLICATION FOR EMPLOYER
IDENTIFICATION NUMBER
(FORM SS-4)

Form **SS-4** (Rev. December 2001) Department of the Treasury Internal Revenue Service	**Application for Employer Identification Number** (For use by employers, corporations, partnerships, trusts, estates, churches, government agencies, Indian tribal entities, certain individuals, and others.) ▶ See separate instructions for each line. ▶ Keep a copy for your records.	EIN OMB No. 1545-0003

<table>
<tr><td rowspan="9" style="writing-mode:vertical-rl">Type or print clearly.</td><td colspan="2">1 Legal name of entity (or individual) for whom the EIN is being requested</td></tr>
<tr><td>2 Trade name of business (if different from name on line 1)</td><td>3 Executor, trustee, "care of" name</td></tr>
<tr><td>4a Mailing address (room, apt., suite no. and street, or P.O. box)</td><td>5a Street address (if different) (Do not enter a P.O. box.)</td></tr>
<tr><td>4b City, state, and ZIP code</td><td>5b City, state, and ZIP code</td></tr>
<tr><td colspan="2">6 County and state where principal business is located</td></tr>
<tr><td>7a Name of principal officer, general partner, grantor, owner, or trustor</td><td>7b SSN, ITIN, or EIN</td></tr>
</table>

8a Type of entity (check only one box)

___ Sole proprietor (SSN) _____ | ___ Estate (SSN of decedent) _____
___ Partnership | ___ Plan administrator (SSN) _____
___ Corporation (enter form number to be filed) ▶ _____ | ___ Trust (SSN of grantor) _____
___ Personal service corp. | ___ National Guard   ___ State/local government
___ Church or church-controlled organization | ___ Farmers' cooperative   ___ Federal government/military
___ Other nonprofit organization (specify) ▶ _____ | ___ REMIC   ___ Indian tribal governments/enterprises
___ Other (specify) ▶ | Group Exemption Number (GEN) ▶ _____

8b If a corporation, name the state or foreign country (if applicable) where incorporated | State | Foreign country

9 **Reason for applying** (check only one box)

___ Started new business (specify type) ▶ _____ | ___ Banking purpose (specify purpose) ▶ _____
| ___ Changed type of organization (specify new type) ▶ _____
| ___ Purchased going business
___ Hired employees (Check the box and see line 12.) | ___ Created a trust (specify type) ▶ _____
___ Compliance with IRS withholding regulations | ___ Created a pension plan (specify type) ▶ _____
___ Other (specify) ▶

10 Date business started or acquired (month, day, year)	**11** Closing month of accounting year

12 First date wages or annuities were paid or will be paid (month, day, year). **Note:** If applicant is a withholding agent, enter date income will first be paid to nonresident alien. (month, day, year) _____ ▶

13 Highest number of employees expected in the next 12 months. **Note:** If the applicant does not expect to have any employees during the period, enter "-0-." _____ ▶	Agricultural	Household	Other

14 Check **one** box that best describes the principal activity of your business. ___ Health care & social assistance   ___ Wholesale-agent/broker
___ Construction   ___ Rental & leasing   ___ Transportation & warehousing   ___ Accommodation & food service   ___ Wholesale-other   ___ Retail
___ Real estate   ___ Manufacturing   ___ Finance & insurance   ___ Other (specify)

15 Indicate principal line of merchandise sold; specific construction work done; products produced; or services provided.

16a Has the applicant ever applied for an employer identification number for this or any other business? _____ ___ Yes   ___ No
Note: If "Yes," please complete lines 16b and 16c.

16b If you checked "Yes" on line 16a, give applicant's legal name and trade name shown on prior application if different from line 1 or 2 above.
Legal name ▶   Trade name ▶

16c Approximate date when, and city and state where, the application was filed. Enter previous employer identification number if known.
Approximate date when filed (mo., day, year) | City and state where filed | Previous EIN

	Complete this section **only** if you want to authorize the named individual to receive the entity's EIN and answer questions about the completion of this form.	
Third Party Designee	Designee's name	Designee's telephone number (include area code) ( )
	Address and ZIP code	Designee's fax number (include area code) ( )

Under penalties of perjury, I declare that I have examined this application, and to the best of my knowledge and belief, it is true, correct, and complete. | Applicant's telephone number (include area code)
( )

Name and title (type or print clearly) ▶

Signature ▶   Date ▶ | Applicant's fax number (include area code)
( )

For Privacy Act and Paperwork Reduction Act Notice, see separate instructions.   Cat. No. 16055N   Form **SS-4** (Rev. 12-2001)

Do I Need an EIN?

File Form SS-4 if the applicant entity does not already have an EIN but is required to show an EIN on any return, statement, or other document.[1] **See also the separate instructions for each line on Form SS-4.**

IF the applicant...	AND...	THEN...
Started a new business	Does not currently have (nor expect to have) employees	Complete lines 1, 2, 4a–6, 8a, and 9–16c.
Hired (or will hire) employees, including household employees	Does not already have an EIN	Complete lines 1, 2, 4a–6, 7a–b (if applicable), 8a, 8b (if applicable), and 9–16c.
Opened a bank account	Needs an EIN for banking purposes only	Complete lines 1–5b, 7a–b (if applicable), 8a, 9, and 16a–c.
Changed type of organization	Either the legal character of the organization or its ownership changed (e.g., you incorporate a sole proprietorship or form a partnership)[2]	Complete lines 1–16c (as applicable).
Purchased a going business[3]	Does not already have an EIN	Complete lines 1–16c (as applicable).
Created a trust	The trust is other than a grantor trust or an IRA trust[4]	Complete lines 1–16c (as applicable).
Created a pension plan as a plan administrator[5]	Needs an EIN for reporting purposes	Complete lines 1, 2, 4a–6, 8a, 9, and 16a–c.
Is a foreign person needing an EIN to comply with IRS withholding regulations	Needs an EIN to complete a Form W-8 (other than Form W-8ECI), avoid withholding on portfolio assets, or claim tax treaty benefits[6]	Complete lines 1–5b, 7a–b (SSN or ITIN optional), 8a–9, and 16a–c.
Is administering an estate	Needs an EIN to report estate income on Form 1041	Complete lines 1, 3, 4a–b, 8a, 9, and 16a–c.
Is a withholding agent for taxes on non-wage income paid to an alien (i.e., individual, corporation, or partnership, etc.)	Is an agent, broker, fiduciary, manager, tenant, or spouse who is required to file **Form 1042,** Annual Withholding Tax Return for U.S. Source Income of Foreign Persons	Complete lines 1, 2, 3 (if applicable), 4a–5b, 7a–b (if applicable), 8a, 9, and 16a–c.
Is a state or local agency	Serves as a tax reporting agent for public assistance recipients under Rev. Proc. 80-4, 1980-1 C.B. 581[7]	Complete lines 1, 2, 4a–5b, 8a, 9, and 16a–c.
Is a single-member LLC	Needs an EIN to file **Form 8832,** Classification Election, for filing employment tax returns, **or** for state reporting purposes[8]	Complete lines 1–16c (as applicable).
Is an S corporation	Needs an EIN to file **Form 2553,** Election by a Small Business Corporation[9]	Complete lines 1–16c (as applicable).

[1] For example, a sole proprietorship or self-employed farmer who establishes a qualified retirement plan, or is required to file excise, employment, alcohol, tobacco, or firearms returns, must have an EIN. **A partnership, corporation, REMIC (real estate mortgage investment conduit), nonprofit organization (church, club, etc.), or farmers' cooperative must use an EIN for any tax-related purpose even if the entity does not have employees.**

[2] However, **do not** apply for a new EIN if the existing entity only **(a)** changed its business name, **(b)** elected on Form 8832 to change the way it is taxed (or is covered by the default rules), or **(c)** terminated its partnership status because at least 50% of the total interests in partnership capital and profits were sold or exchanged within a 12-month period. (The EIN of the terminated partnership should continue to be used. See Regulations section 301.6109- 1(d)(2)(iii).)

[3] Do not use the EIN of the prior business unless you became the "owner" of a corporation by acquiring its stock.

[4] However, IRA trusts that are required to file **Form 990-T,** Exempt Organization Business Income Tax Return, must have an EIN.

[5] A plan administrator is the person or group of persons specified as the administrator by the instrument under which the plan is operated.

[6] Entities applying to be a Qualified Intermediary (QI) need a QI-EIN even if they already have an EIN. **See Rev. Proc. 2000-12.**

[7] See also Household employer on page 4. (**Note:** State or local agencies may need an EIN for other reasons, e.g., hired employees.)

[8] Most LLCs **do not** need to file Form 8832. See **Limited liability company (LLC)** on page 4 for details on completing Form SS-4 for an LLC.

[9] An existing corporation that is electing or revoking S corporation status should use its previously-assigned EIN.

APPENDIX 30:
THE BETTER BUSINESS BUREAU CODE OF ONLINE BUSINESS PRACTICES

INTRODUCTION

1. The following Code of Online Business Practices is designed to guide ethical "business to customer" conduct in electronic commerce. These guidelines represent sound online advertising and selling practices that the Better Business Bureau ("BBB") and BBBOnLine believe will boost customer trust and confidence in online commerce.

2. This Code serves two purposes:

(a) First, the Code provides desirable standards for e-commerce generally. Adherence to the provisions of this Code will be a significant contribution toward effective self-regulation in the public interest. We urge online businesses to comply with the Code and to establish the necessary management procedures that will assure success.

(b) Second, it is the underpinning for the BBBOnLine Reliability Program and all Reliability participants must agree to follow it and to dispute resolution, at the customer's request, for unresolved disputes involving products or services advertised or purchased online. Online businesses that are or become Reliability participants will be able to demonstrate to the public their commitment to the Code's good business practices by displaying the Reliability Seal.

3. The Code contains practical, performance-based guidelines, rather than dictating methods for achieving the goals that could interfere with particular business models. While the Code establishes goals for the online business, it does not dictate how these goals should be reached, leaving those decisions up to the online business that knows its business model best. As such, the Code is designed to allow online businesses to take advantage of evolving technology and to foster innovation while adhering to principled business practices that provide truthful and accurate information to online customers.

4. The Code uses the term "should" in recognition that this is a voluntary code. However, all provisions are recommended for implementation by the online business community.

5. BBB and BBBOnLine encourage online businesses, to the extent they target particular geographic markets or countries with their online advertising or marketing, to consider the targeted geographical markets' or countries' regulatory requirements. However, the Code does not address whether the laws, if any, of any particular jurisdiction apply to online advertising or transactions. Online businesses are therefore advised to make a determination that their practices are in compliance with applicable laws.

6. E-commerce is developing at a rapid pace and BBB and BBBOnLine recognize that this Code may need to be modified over time to keep it current with developing technology, new business models, and customer needs. BBB and BBBOnLine are committed to review the Code and update it as needed.

7. Terms:

(a) Online Advertiser: A person or entity acts as an "online advertiser" when it promotes its own goods or services on the Internet. Therefore, code provisions referring to online advertisers apply when the business is acting as an online advertiser for a particular activity. If in certain situations an online advertiser acts as an online merchant, then in those situations, it must also comply with the online merchant Code requirements.

(b) Online Merchant: A person or entity acts as an "online merchant" when it offers its own goods and services online and accepts online orders. A business may act as an online merchant in certain situations but not in others. Therefore, Code provisions referring to online merchants apply when the business is acting as an online merchant for a particular activity. All online merchants are also online advertisers and as such, should adhere to online advertiser Code provisions as well.

(c) Purchase: For purposes of this Code, the term "purchase" is intended to be used broadly and is meant to include other transactions, including but not limited to, leasing, licensing or barter.

PRINCIPLES FOR ETHICAL BUSINESS TO CUSTOMER CONDUCT

The following statements represent the five principles upon which this Code is based.

PRINCIPLE I: TRUTHFUL AND ACCURATE COMMUNICATION

Online advertisers should not engage in deceptive or misleading trade practices with regard to any aspect of electronic commerce, including advertising, marketing, or in their use of technology.

A. Online advertisers should adhere to the Better Business Bureau's Code of Advertising. Online advertisers should engage in truthful advertising. They should not make deceptive or misleading representations or omissions of material facts.

1. Online advertisers should be able to substantiate any express or reasonably implied factual claims made in their advertising or marketing and should possess reasonable substantiation prior to disseminating a claim.

2. Online advertisers should disclose their advertising or marketing to be such if failure to do so would be misleading.

(a) For example, if material information in an advertisement appears misleading because it is difficult to distinguish between editorial content and advertising, the advertising should be labeled as such.

(b) Likewise, online advertisers should not disguise advertising as technical or desktop functionality when doing so would mislead customers into clicking on the advertisement thinking that they were actually performing a technical function.

3. If online advertisers make price comparisons, they should disclose the basis for, or the geographic area that constitutes, the market area. In all cases, online advertisers should either disclose the date when the comparison was made or if they offer ongoing claims, keep the substantiation current.

4. Online advertisers should cooperate with any bona fide, industry self-regulatory advertising programs where such programs exist to resolve any advertising disputes.

B. Online advertisers should use Internet technology to promote the customer's knowledge of the products or services being offered and should not use technology to mislead customers.

1. Online advertisers should not mislead online customers by creating the false impression of sponsorship, endorsement, popularity, trustworthiness, product quality or business size through the misuse of hyperlinks, "seals", other technology, or another's intellectual property.

2. Online advertisers may use hyperlinks to add to or supplement information about goods or services but should not misleadingly use hyperlinks or information provided via a hyperlink to:

(a) contradict or substantially change the meaning of any material statement or claim;

(b) create the false impression of affiliation;

(c) create the false impression that the content, merchandise or service of another's business is their own.

3. Online advertisers should only use search terms or mechanisms that fairly reflect the content of their site.

4. Online advertisers should make sure that any third-party "seals" or endorsements that incorporate links to self-regulatory or ethical standard programs are functional so that customers can easily verify membership in the seal program and determine its purpose, scope, and standards. Any online advertiser that participates in any third-party self-regulatory or ethical standard or seal program should do so in conformity with that program's instructions regarding the display, activation, and uses of the seal or endorsement. If an express or implied claim is made through the use of a seal or text, the online advertiser should provide customers with the opportunity to understand the details behind the program, including the program's claims, scope and standards.

5. Online advertisers should not knowingly link to, or accept affinity or royalty payments from, deceptive, fraudulent, or illegal sites.

6. Online advertisers should not deceptively interfere with a customer's browser, computer, or any appliance the customer uses to access the Internet.

PRINCIPLE II: DISCLOSURE

Online merchants should disclose to their customers and prospective customers information about the business, the goods or services available for purchase online, and the transaction itself.

A. All information required by this Code should meet the following standards:

1. It should be clear, accurate, and easy to find and understand;

2. It should be readily accessible online and can appear via a noticeable and descriptive hyperlink or other similarly effective mechanism;

3. It should be presented such that customers can access and maintain an adequate record of it;

4. And, if the information relates to the goods or services available for purchase online or the transaction itself, it should be accessible prior to the consummation of the transaction.

B. Information About the Business:

1. Online merchants should provide, at a minimum, the following contact information online:

(a) legal name;

(b) the name under which it conducts business;

(c) the principle physical address or information, including country, sufficient to ensure the customer can locate the business offline;

(d) an online method of contact such as e-mail;

(e) a point of contact within the organization that is responsible for customer inquires; and

(f) a telephone number unless to do so would be disruptive to the operation of the business given its size and resources and then, the merchant should maintain a working listed phone number.

2. Online merchants that register an Internet domain name should provide complete and accurate information to the authorized Internet registrar with which they register and should use the appropriate top-level domain for the type of business registered.

C. Information About Goods and Services Available for Purchase Online: Online merchants should provide enough information available about the goods or services available online so that customers can make an informed choice about whether to purchase such goods or services.

D. Information About the Online Transaction Itself: Online merchants should provide enough information about the online transaction itself so that customers can make an informed choice about whether to engage in the online transaction.

1. Online merchants should disclose material information about the online transaction itself including, but not limited to:

(a) terms of the transaction

(b) product availability/shipping information; and

(c) prices and customer costs.

2. And should provide the customer with an opportunity to:

(a) review and approve the transaction and

(b) receive a confirmation.

3. If the online merchant chooses to provide some information in more than one language, all material information about the transaction should be available in the selected languages. Similarly, if the online merchant chooses to reach a particular population, such as the aged or handicapped, by using large font sizes or specific colors for example, all material information about the transaction should be provided in the same way.

E. Terms of the Online Transaction: Online merchants should provide the terms of the online transaction including but not limited to:

1. Any restrictions or limitations (for example, time or geographic) they impose on the sale of the goods or services;

2. Easy-to-use payment mechanisms;

3. Return or refund policies, including how customers can make returns or exchanges; obtain refunds or credits; or cancel a transaction; and any associated time limitations or associated fees;

4. For products, any warrantees, guarantees, escrow programs or other offered terms, including limitations, conditions, if any;

5. For services, any material standards, schedules, fees, or other offered terms, including limitation and conditions;

6. For contests, sweepstakes or other similar promotions, the complete rules adjacent to, or in a hyperlink or similar technology adjacent to, the promotion itself; and

7. For ongoing transactions or subscriptions:

(a) information about how the transaction will appear on the bill so that the customer can easily identify the business and the transaction on the bill;

(b) easy-to-understand cancellation information, an easy to use means to cancel an ongoing subscription, and timely confirmation of such cancellation.

F. Product Availability/Terms of Shipping: Online merchants should:

1. Note which products or services are temporarily unavailable and in those instances:

(a) provide information about when the customer will be charged for the transaction; and

(b) if an expected availability date is provided for unavailable products or services, have a reasonable basis for such date.

2. Have a reasonable basis for, and provide customers with, estimated shipping times (or in the case of online delivery, delivery times) (if such times are unknown at the time of the online transaction, the online merchant should provide the information via a timely follow-up e-mail but should provide the customer with the opportunity to cancel the transaction if the time indicated is unacceptable);

3. Have a reasonable basis for stated delivery claims when made;

4. Disclose any shipping, performance, or delivery limitations they impose (age, geographic); and

5. If a material delay in shipping or performance occurs, provide the customer with timely information about the delay and the opportunity to cancel the transaction.

G. Prices and Customer Costs: Online merchants should:

1. Disclose, in a specified currency, an itemized list of the prices or fees and expected customer costs to be collected by the online merchant with regard to an online transaction, including but not limited to:

(a) price or license fee to be charged, or in the case of a barter trade, the items that will be exchanged for goods or services purchased or licensed;

(b) expected shipping and handling charges (if such charges are unknown at the time of the online transaction, the online merchant should provide the information via a timely follow-up e-mail but should provide the customer with the opportunity to cancel the transaction if the costs are unacceptable); and

(c) expected taxes or other government imposed fees collected by the online merchant related to the transaction, etc.;

2. Provide a generalized description of other routine costs and fees related to the transaction that may be incurred by the cus-

tomer such as tariffs or routine subscription fees that may not be collected by the online merchant;

3. Clearly identify the merchant's name and website address on any subsequent statements or other billing information; and

4. Honor the amount authorized by the customer in any subsequent bills to the customer.

H. Provide Opportunity to Review and Approve Transaction Prior to completion of the transaction, online merchants should provide customers with the option to review the online transaction and to confirm their intent to enter into the transaction by providing a summary that includes:

1. Information about the online transaction (as outlined in sections above);

2. The selected payment method; and

3. The option to cancel or affirmatively complete the transaction.

I. Provide Confirmation of the Sale: Online merchants should provide customers with the option to receive a confirmation of the transaction after the transaction has been completed. The confirmation should include:

1. A line-itemed statement of what was ordered, the price, and any other known charges such as shipping/handling and taxes,

2. Sufficient contact information to enable purchasers to obtain order status updates, and

3. The anticipated date of shipment. Online merchants should disclose to their customers and prospective customers information about the business, the goods or services available for purchase online, and the transaction itself.

PRINCIPLE III: INFORMATION PRACTICES AND SECURITY

Online advertisers should adopt information practices that treat customers' personal information with care. They should post and adhere to a privacy policy based on fair information principles, take appropriate measures to provide adequate security, and respect customers' preferences regarding unsolicited email.

A. Post and Adhere to a Privacy Policy Online advertisers should post and adhere to a privacy policy that is open, transparent, and meets generally accepted fair information principles including providing notice as to what personal information the online advertiser collects, uses, and discloses; what choices customers have with regard to the business' collection, use and, disclosure of that information; what access customers have to the information; what security measures are taken to protect the information, and what enforcement and redress mechanisms are in place to remedy any violations of the policy. The privacy policy should be easy to find and understand and be available prior to or at the time the customer provides any personally identifiable information.

B. Provide Adequate Security Online advertisers should use appropriate levels of security for the type of information collected, maintained, or transferred to third parties and should:

1. Use industry standard levels of encryption and authentication for the transfer or receipt of health care information, social security numbers, financial transaction information (for example, a credit card number), or other sensitive information;

2. Provide industry standard levels of security and integrity to protect data being maintained by computers; and

3. Take reasonable steps to require third parties involved in fulfilling a customer transaction to also maintain appropriate levels of security.

C. Respect Customer's Preferences Regarding Unsolicited E-mail: Online advertisers should accurately describe their business practices with regard to their use of unsolicited e-mail to customers.

1. Online advertisers that engage in unsolicited email marketing should post and adhere to a "Do Not Contact" policy—a policy that, at a minimum, enables those customers who do not wish to be contacted online to "opt out" online from future solicitations. This policy should be available both on the website and in any emails, other than those relating to a particular order.

2. Online advertisers that engage in unsolicited email marketing should also subscribe to a bona-fide e-mail suppression list such as ones offered by Center for Democracy and Technology at http://opt-out.cdt.org and the Direct Marketing Association at http://www.e-mps.org/en.

PRINCIPLE IV: CUSTOMER SATISFACTION

Online merchants should seek to ensure their customers are satisfied by honoring their representations, answering questions, and resolving customer complaints and disputes in a timely and responsive manner.

A. Honor Representations: Online merchants should comply with all commitments, representations, and other promises made to a customer.

B. Answer Questions: Online merchants should provide an easy-to-find and understand notice of how customers can successfully and meaningfully contact the business to get answers to their questions. Online merchants should promptly and substantively respond to the customer's commercially reasonable questions.

C. Resolve Customer Complaints and Disputes: Online merchants should seek to resolve customer complaints and disputes in a fair, timely, and effective manner.

1. Online merchants should provide an easy-to-find and understandable notice of how a customer can successfully and meaningfully contact the business to expeditiously resolve complaints and disputes related to a transaction.

2. Online merchants shall have an effective and easy to use internal mechanism for addressing complaints and correcting errors. Examples include fair exchange policies, return policies, etc.

3. In the event the customer's complaint cannot be resolved, online merchants shall also offer a fair method for resolving differences with regard to a transaction by offering either an unconditional money-back guarantee or third-party dispute resolution.

(a) If an online merchant offers third party dispute resolution, it should use a trusted third party that offers impartial, accessible, and timely arbitration that is free to consumers or at a charge to consumers that is not disproportionate to the value of goods or services involved in the dispute.

(b) Online merchants should provide customers with easy-to-find and understandable contact information for such third parties, including a link (or similar technology) to any third party sites used for such means.

PRINCIPLE V: PROTECTING CHILDREN

If online advertisers target children under the age of 13, they should take special care to protect children by recognizing their developing cognitive abilities.

A. Online advertisers should adhere to the Children's Advertising Review Unit's ("CARU") Self Regulatory Guidelines for Children's Advertising.

B. Specifically, online advertisers should adhere to the Guidelines for Interactive Electronic Media that apply to online activities, which are intentionally targeted to children under 13, or where the website knows the visitor is a child. These Guidelines include parental permission first requirements in the "Making a Sale" and "Data Collection" provisions.

GLOSSARY

ACCOUNTS PAYABLE—Trade accounts of businesses representing obligations to pay for goods and services received.

ACCOUNTS RECEIVABLE—Trade accounts of businesses representing moneys due for goods sold or services rendered evidenced by notes, statements, invoices or other written evidence of a present obligation.

ACCOUNTING—The recording, classifying, summarizing and interpreting in a significant manner and in terms of money, transactions and events of a financial character.

ADHESION CONTRACT—A standardized contract form offered to consumers of goods and services on a "take it or leave it" basis without affording the consumer a realistic opportunity to bargain, and under such conditions that infer coercion.

AGENCY—The relationship between a principal and an agent who is employed by the principal, to perform certain acts dealing with third parties.

AGENT—One who represents another known as the principal.

ANTITRUST LAWS—Statutes designed to promote free competition in the market place.

APPARENT AGENCY—Apparent agency exists when one person, whether or not authorized, reasonably appears to a third person to be authorized to act as agent for such other.

ARBITRATION—The reference of a dispute to an impartial person chosen by the parties to the dispute who agree in advance to abide by the arbitrator's award issued after a hearing at which both parties have an opportunity to be heard.

ARBITRATION ACTS—Federal and state laws which provide for submission of disputes to the process of arbitration.

ARBITRATION BOARD—A panel of arbitrators appointed to hear and decide a dispute according to the rules of arbitration.

ARBITRATION CLAUSE—A clause inserted in a contract providing for compulsory arbitration in case of a dispute as to the rights or liabilities under such contract.

ARBITRATOR—A private, disinterested person, chosen by the parties to a disputed question, for the purpose of hearing their contention, and awarding judgment to the prevailing party.

ARM'S LENGTH—Refers to the bargaining position of two parties that are unrelated to one another and have no other motivation for dealing other than to transact business in good faith.

ASSUMPTION—The act of assuming/undertaking another's debts or obligations.

AUCTION—A public sale of goods to the highest bidder.

AUTOMATIC DATA PROCESSING—Data processing largely performed by automatic means.

BALANCE SHEET—A report of the status of a firm's assets, liabilities and owner's equity at a given time.

BAD FAITH—A willful failure to comply with one's statutory or contractual obligations.

BANKRUPTCY—A condition in which a business cannot meet its debt obligations and petitions a federal district court for either reorganization of its debts or liquidation of its assets.

BID—An offer to buy goods or services at a stated price.

BILATERAL CONTRACT—A bilateral contract is one containing mutual promises between the parties to the contract, each being termed both a promisor and a promisee.

BILL—In commercial law, an account for goods sold, services rendered and work done.

BILL OF LADING—In commercial law, the document given to the shipper by the carrier in connection with goods to be transported by the carrier.

BILL OF SALE—A written agreement by which the exchange of personal property is made.

BOARD OF DIRECTORS—The governing body of a corporation which is elected by the stockholders.

BOILERPLATE—Refers to standard language found almost universally in certain documents.

BREACH OF CONTRACT—The failure, without any legal excuse, to perform any promise which forms the whole or the part of a contract.

BREACH OF WARRANTY—An infraction of an express or implied agreement as to the title, quality, content or condition of a thing which is sold.

BREAK-EVEN POINT—The break-even point in any business is that point at which the volume of sales or revenues exactly equals total expenses —i.e., the point at which there is neither a profit nor loss.

BULK SALES ACT —Statutes designed to prevent the defrauding of a merchant's creditors by the secret bulk sale of substantially all of the merchant's stock.

BULK TRANSFER—A type of commercial fraud wherein a merchant transfers all or most of the business, for consideration, without paying creditors from the proceeds of the sale.

BUSINESS BIRTH—Formation of a new establishment or enterprise.

BUSINESS DEATH—Voluntary or involuntary closure of a firm or establishment.

BUSINESS DISSOLUTION—For enumeration purposes, the absence from any current record of a business that was present in a prior time period.

BUSINESS FAILURE—The closure of a business causing a loss to at least one creditor.

BUSINESS INFORMATION CENTER (BIC)—One of more than 50 specialized Small Business Administration units which offer the latest in high-technology hard-ware, software and telecommunications to assist small business and one-on-one counseling with seasoned business veterans through the Service Corps of Retired Executives (SCORE).

BUSINESS PLAN—A comprehensive planning document which clearly describes the business developmental objective of an existing or proposed business and outlines what and how and from where the resources needed to accomplish the objective will be obtained and utilized.

BUSINESS START—For enumeration purposes, a business with a name or similar designation that did not exist in a prior time period.

CANCELED LOAN—The annulment or rescission of an approved loan prior to disbursement.

CAPITAL—Assets less liabilities, representing the ownership interest in a business.

CAPITAL CONTRIBUTION—Cash, property or services contributed by partners to a partnership.

CAPITAL EXPENDITURES—Business spending on additional equipment and inventory.

CAPITAL GAIN—The excess of proceeds over cost, or other basis, from the sale of a capital asset.

CAPITAL LOSS—Loss on the sale or exchange of a capital asset.

CAPITALIZED PROPERTY—Personal property of the business which has an average dollar value of $300.00 or more and a life expectancy of one year or more.

CASH DISCOUNT—An incentive offered by the seller to encourage the buyer to pay within a stipulated time.

CASH FLOW—The amount of funds a business receives during any given period minus what is paid out during the same period.

CHARGE-OFF—An accounting transaction removing an uncollectible balance from the active receivable accounts.

CHARGED OFF LOAN—An uncollectible loan for which the principal and accrued interest were removed from the receivable accounts.

CHARTER—The document issued by the government establishing a corporate entity.

CLAYTON ACT—A federal statute amending the Sherman Antitrust Act.

CLOSE CORPORATION—A corporation whose shares, or at least voting shares, are held by a single shareholder or closely-knit group of shareholders.

CLOSED LOAN—Any loan for which funds have been disbursed, and all required documentation has been executed, received and reviewed.

CLOSING—Actions and procedures required to effect the documentation and disbursement of loan funds after the application has been approved, and the execution of all required documentation and its filing and recordation where required.

COLLATERAL—Something of value—securities, evidence of deposit or other property—pledged to support the repayment of an obligation.

COLLATERAL DOCUMENT—A legal document covering the item(s) pledged as collateral on a loan, i.e., note, mortgages, assignment, etc.

COMMINGLE—To combine funds or properties into a common fund.

COMPROMISE—The settlement of a claim resulting from a defaulted loan for less than the full amount due.

COMPULSORY ARBITRATION—Arbitration which occurs when the consent of one of the parties is enforced by statutory provisions.

CONSOLIDATION—A combination of two or more corporations which are succeeded by a new corporation, usually with a new title.

CONSORTIUM—A coalition of organizations, such as banks and corporations, set up to fund ventures requiring large capital resources.

CONSUMER CREDIT—Loans and sale credit extended to individuals to finance the purchases of goods and services arising out of consumer needs and desires.

CONTINGENT LIABILITY—A potential obligation that may be incurred dependent upon the occurrence of a future event.

CONTRACT—A contract is an agreement between two or more persons which creates an obligation to do or not to do a particular thing.

CORPORATION—A group of persons granted a state charter legally recognizing them as a separate entity having its own rights, privileges, and liabilities distinct from those of its members.

COSTS—Money obligated for goods and services received during a given period of time, regardless of when ordered or whether paid for.

CREDIT RATING—A grade assigned to a business concern to denote the net worth and credit standing to which the concern is entitled in the opinion of the rating agency as a result of its investigation.

DEBENTURE—Debt instrument evidencing the holder's right to receive interest and principal installments from the named obligor.

DEBT CAPITAL—Business financing that normally requires periodic interest payments and repayment of the principal within a specified time.

DEBT FINANCING—The provision of long-term loans to small business concerns in exchange for debt securities or a note.

DEED OF TRUST—A document under seal which, when delivered, transfers a present interest in property and may be held as collateral.

DEFAULTS—The nonpayment of principal and/or interest on the due date as provided by the terms and conditions of the note.

DEFERRED LOAN—Loans whose principal and or interest installments are postponed for a specified period of time.

DEMAND FOR ARBITRATION—A unilateral filing of a claim in arbitration based on the filer's contractual or statutory right to do so.

DISCLAIMER—Words or conduct which tend to negate or limit warranty in the sale of goods, which in certain instances must be conspicuous and refer to the specific warranty to be excluded.

DIVESTITURE—Change of ownership and/or control of a business from a majority to disadvantaged persons.

DOMESTIC CORPORATION—In reference to a particular state, a domestic corporation is one created by, or organized under, the laws of that state.

DRAM SHOP ACT—Refers to laws which impose strict liability upon the seller of intoxicating beverages when harm is caused to a third party as a result of the sale.

EARNING POWER—The demonstrated ability of a business to earn a profit, over time, while following good accounting practices.

ENTERPRISE—Aggregation of all establishments owned by a parent company, which may consist of a single, independent establishment or subsidiaries or other branch establishments under the same ownership and control.

ENTREPRENEUR—One who assumes the financial risk of the initiation, operation and management of a given business or undertaking.

EQUITY—An ownership interest in a business.

EQUITY FINANCING—The provision of funds for capital or operating expenses in exchange for capital stock, stock purchase warrants and options in the business financed, without any guaranteed return, but with the opportunity to share in the company's profits.

EQUITY PARTNERSHIP—A limited partnership arrangement for providing start-up and seed capital to businesses.

ESCROW ACCOUNT—Funds placed in trust with a third party, by a borrower for a specific purpose and to be delivered to the borrower only upon the fulfillment of certain conditions.

ESTABLISHMENT—A single-location business unit, which may be independent—called a single-establishment enterprise—or owned by a parent enterprise.

FACTORING—A method of financing accounts receivable wherein a firm sells its accounts receivable to a financial institution.

FEATHERBEDDING—An unfair labor practice whereby the time spent, or number of employees needed, to complete a particular task, is increased unnecessarily for the purpose of creating employment.

FEDERAL TRADE COMMISSION—The Federal Trade Commission is an agency of the federal government created in 1914 for the purpose of promoting free and fair competition in interstate commerce through the prevention of general trade restraints.

FINANCE CHARGE—Any charge for an extension of credit, such as interest.

FINANCIAL REPORTS—Reports commonly required from applicants who request financial assistance such as balance sheets, income statements and cash flow charts.

FINANCING—New funds provided to a business, by either loans or purchase of debt securities or capital stock.

FISCAL YEAR—Any twelve-month period used by a business as its fiscal accounting period.

FIXED CAPITAL—The amount of money permanently invested in a business.

FLOW CHART—A graphical representation for the definition, analysis, or solution of a problem, in which symbols are used to represent operations, data, flow, equipment, etc.

FORCE MAJEURE—Force majeure is a clause commonly found in construction contracts which protects the parties in the event that a part of the contract cannot be performed due to causes which are outside the control of the parties.

FORECLOSURE—The act by the mortgagee or trustee upon default, in the payment of interest or principal of a mortgage of enforcing payment of the debt by selling the underlying security.

FOREIGN CORPORATION—In reference to a particular state, a foreign corporation is one created by or under the laws of another state, government or country.

FRANCHISING—A form of business by which the owner—i.e., the franchisor—of a product, service or method obtains distribution through affiliated dealers—i.e., the franchisees—and whereby the product, method or service being marketed is usually identified by the franchisor's brand name, and the franchisee is often given exclusive access to a defined geographical area as well as assistance in organizing, training, merchandising, marketing and managing in return for a consideration.

FREE ON BOARD (FOB)—Free on board is a commercial term that signifies a contractual agreement between a buyer and a seller to have the subject of a sale delivered to a designated place, usually either the place of shipment or the place of destination.

GARNISH—To attach a portion of the wages or other property of a debtor to secure repayment of the debt.

GARNISHEE—A person who receives notice to hold the assets of another, which are in his or her possession, until such time as a court orders the disposition of the property.

GENERAL PARTNER—A partner who participates fully in the profits, losses and management of the partnership, and who is personally liable for its debts.

GENERAL PARTNERSHIP—A type of partnership in which all of the partners share the profits and losses as well as the management fully, though their capital contributions may vary.

GRACE PERIOD—In contract law, a period specified in a contract which is beyond the due date but during which time payment will be accepted without penalty.

GROSS DOMESTIC PRODUCT (GDP)—The most comprehensive single measure of aggregate economic output representing the market value of the total output of the goods and services produced by a nation's economy.

GUARANTEED LOAN—A loan made and serviced by a lending institution under agreement that a governmental agency will purchase the guaranteed portion if the borrower defaults.

HAZARD INSURANCE—Insurance required showing lender as loss payee covering certain risks on real and personal property used for securing loans.

IMPOSSIBILITY—Impossibility is a defense to breach of contract and arises when performance is impossible due to the destruction of the subject matter of the contract or the death of a person necessary for performance.

INCOME STATEMENT—A report of revenue and expenses which shows the results of business operations or net income for a specified period of time.

INCORPORATION—To form a corporation by following established legal procedures.

INDEMNIFICATION CLAUSE—An indemnification clause in a contract refers to the agreement by one party to secure the other party against loss or damage which may occur in the future in connection with performance of the contract.

INDEMNIFY—To hold another harmless for loss or damage which has already occurred, or which may occur in the future.

INDUSTRIAL REVENUE BOND (IRB)—A tax-exempt bond issued by a state or local government agency to finance industrial or commercial projects that serve a public good. The bond usually is not backed by the full faith and credit of the government that issues it, but is repaid solely from the revenues of the project and requires a private sector commitment for repayment.

INNOVATION—Introduction of a new idea into the marketplace in the form of a new product or service, or an improvement in organization or process.

INSOLVENCY—The inability of a borrower to meet financial obligations as they mature, or having insufficient assets to pay legal debts.

INSTALLMENT CONTRACT—An installment contract is one in which the obligation, such as the payment of money, is divided into a series of successive performances over a period of time.

INTEREST—An amount paid a lender for the use of funds.

INVESTMENT BANKING—Businesses specializing in the formation of capital.

JOB DESCRIPTION—A written statement listing the elements of a particular job or occupation, e.g., purpose, duties, equipment used, qualifications, training, physical and mental demands, working conditions, etc.

JUDGMENT—Judicial determination of the existence of an indebtedness, or other legal liability.

JUDGMENT BY CONFESSION—The act of debtors permitting judgment to be entered against them for a given sum with a statement to that effect, without the institution of legal proceedings.

JUDGMENT CREDITOR—A creditor who has obtained a judgment against a debtor, which judgment may be enforced to obtain payment of the amount due.

JUDGMENT DEBTOR—An individual who owes a sum of money, and against whom a judgment has been awarded for that debt.

JUNK BOND—A high-yield corporate bond issue with a below-investment rating that became a growing source of corporate funding in the 1980s.

LABOR ORGANIZATION—An association of workers for the purpose of bargaining the terms and conditions of employment on behalf of labor and management.

LEASE—A contract between an owner—i.e., a lessor—and a tenant—i.e., a lessee—stating the conditions under which the tenant may occupy or use the property.

LEGAL RATE OF INTEREST—The maximum rate of interest fixed by the laws of the various states, which a lender may charge a borrower for the use of money.

LENDING INSTITUTION—Any institution, including a commercial bank, savings and loan association, commercial finance company, or other lender qualified to participate in the making of loans.

LETTER OF INTENT—A non-binding writing intended to set forth the intentions between parties in anticipation of a formal, binding contract.

LEVERAGED BUY-OUT—The purchase of a business, with financing provided largely by borrowed money, often in the form of junk bonds.

LIEN—A charge upon or security interest in real or personal property maintained to ensure the satisfaction of a debt or duty ordinarily arising by operation of law.

LIMITED PARTNER—A partner whose participation in the profits of the business is limited by agreement and who is not liable for the debts of the partnership beyond his or her capital contribution.

LIMITED PARTNERSHIP—A type of partnership comprised of one or more general partners who manage the business and who are personally liable for partnership debts, and one or more limited partners who contribute capital and share in profits but who take no part in running the business and incur no liability with respect to partnership obligations beyond contribution.

LINE OF CREDIT—An arrangement whereby a financial institution commits itself to lend up to a specified maximum amount of funds during a specified period.

LIQUIDATED DAMAGES—An amount stipulated in a contract as a reasonable estimate of damages to be paid in the event the contract is breached.

LIQUIDATION—The disposal, at maximum prices, of the collateral securing a loan, and the voluntary and enforced collection of the remaining loan balance from the obligators and/or guarantors.

LIQUIDATION VALUE—The net value realizable in the sale—ordinarily a forced sale—of a business or a particular asset.

LITIGATION—The practice of taking legal action through the judicial process.

LOAN AGREEMENT—Agreement to be executed by borrower, containing pertinent terms, conditions, covenants and restrictions.

LOAN PAYOFF AMOUNT—The total amount of money needed to meet a borrower's obligation on a loan.

LOSS RATE—A rate developed by comparing the ratio of total loans charged off to the total loans disbursed from inception of the program to the present date.

MARKET—The set of existing and prospective users of a product or service.

MARKET PENETRATION—A systematic campaign to increase sales in current markets of an existing product or service.

MARKET SEGMENT—A distinct or definable subset of a target market.

MARKUP—Markup is the difference between invoice cost and selling price which may be expressed either as a percentage of the selling price or the cost price and is supposed to cover all the costs of doing business plus a profit.

MATERIAL BREACH—A material breach refers to a substantial breach of contract which excuses further performance by the innocent party and gives rise to an action for breach of contract by the injured party.

MATURITY—As applied to securities and commercial paper, the period end date when payment of principal is due.

MATURITY EXTENSIONS—Extensions of payment beyond the original period established for repayment of a loan.

MECHANIC'S LIEN—A claim created by law for the purpose of securing a priority of payment of the price of work performed and materials used.

MERGER—A combination of two or more corporations wherein the dominant unit absorbs the passive ones, and the former continuing operation usually under the same name.

MEDIATION—The act of a third person in intermediating between two contending parties with a view to persuading them to adjust or settle their dispute but without the authority to make a binding decision.

MEDIATOR—One who interposes between parties at variance for the purpose of reconciling them.

NATIONAL LABOR RELATIONS BOARD—An independent agency created by the National Labor Relations Act of 1935 (Wagner Act), as amended by the acts of 1947 (Taft-Hartley Act) and 1959 (Landrum-Griffin Act), established to regulate the relations between employers and employees.

NEGOTIATION—In labor law, refers to the "face to face" process used by local unions and the employer to exchange their views on those matters involving personnel policies and practices, or other matters affecting the working conditions of employees.

NEGOTIATION DISPUTE—That point in negotiations where labor and management cannot come to an agreement on some or all of the issues on the bargaining table.

NEGOTIATED GRIEVANCE PROCEDURE—The sole and exclusive procedure available to all employees in a particular bargaining unit and the employer for processing grievances and disputes.

NET ASSETS—Total assets minus total liabilities.

NET INCOME—The excess of all revenues and gains for a period over all expenses and losses of the same period.

NET LOSS—The excess of all expenses and losses for a period over all revenues and gains of the same period.

NET WORTH—Property owned, i.e. — assets — minus debts and obligations owed—i.e., liabilities—is the owner's net worth—i.e., equity.

NOTES AND ACCOUNTS RECEIVABLE—A secured or unsecured receivable evidenced by a note or open account arising from activities involving liquidation and disposal of loan collateral.

ORDINARY INTEREST—Simple interest based on a year of 360 days, contrasting with exact interest having a base year of 365 days.

ORGANIZATIONAL CHART—A linear direction of responsibility and authority within a company or institution.

OUTLAYS—Net disbursements for administrative expenses and for loans and related costs and expenses.

PARTNERSHIP—A legal relationship existing between two or more persons contractually associated as joint principals in a business.

PATENT—A patent secures the exclusive right to make, use and sell an invention for 17 years.

PIERCING THE CORPORATE VEIL—The process of holding another liable, such as an individual, for the acts of a corporation.

PRIME RATE—Interest rate which is charged business borrowers having the highest credit ratings, for short-term borrowing.

PRODUCT LIABILITY—Type of tort or civil liability that applies to product manufacturers and sellers.

PROFESSIONAL ASSOCIATIONS—Non-profit, cooperative and voluntary organizations that are designed to help their members in dealing with problems of mutual interest.

PROFESSIONAL MALPRACTICE—The failure of one rendering professional services to exercise that degree of skill and learning commonly applied in the community by the average prudent reputable member of the profession, with the result of injury, loss or damage to the recipient of those services, or to those entitled to rely upon them.

PROFIT—Excess of revenues over expenses for a transaction.

PROFIT AND LOSS STATEMENT—Statement of income.

PROFIT MARGIN—Sales minus all expenses.

PROPRIETORSHIP—The most common legal form of business ownership comprising about 85 percent of all small businesses and whereby the liability of the owner is unlimited.

PRO-RATA BASIS—Proportionately.

PROSPECTUS—A document given by a company to prospective investors, which sets forth all the material information concerning the company and its financial stability, so the investor can make an informed decision on whether to invest in it.

PURCHASE ORDER—A document which authorizes a seller to deliver goods, and is considered an offer which is accepted upon delivery.

RATIO—Denotes relationships of items within and between financial statements, e.g., current ratio, quick ratio, inventory turnover ratio and debt/net worth ratios.

REFORMATION—An equitable remedy which calls for the rewriting of a contract involving a mutual mistake or fraud.

RESCISSION—The cancellation of a contract which returns the parties to the positions they were in before the contract was made.

RETURN ON INVESTMENT—The amount of profit—i.e., return—based on the amount of resources—i.e., funds—used to produce it.

SALE—An agreement to transfer property from the seller to the buyer for a stated sum of money.

SALE AND LEASEBACK—An agreement whereby the seller transfers property to the buyer who immediately leases the property back to the seller.

SCOPE OF EMPLOYMENT—Those activities performed while carrying out the business of one's employer.

SECONDARY MARKET—Those who purchase an interest in a loan from an original lender, such as banks, institutional investors, insurance companies, credit unions and pension funds.

SERVICE CORPS OF RETIRED EXECUTIVES (SCORE)—Retired, and working, successful business persons who volunteer to render assistance in counseling, training and guiding small business clients.

SHAREHOLDER—A person who owns shares of stock in a corporation or joint-stock company, also referred to as a stockholder.

SHERMAN ANTITRUST ACT—A federal statute passed in 1890 to prohibit monopolization and unreasonable restraint of trade in interstate and foreign commerce.

SILENT PARTNER—An investor in a business who is either unidentified to third parties, or who does not take an active role in day-to-day management of the business.

SMALL BUSINESS DEVELOPMENT CENTER (SBDC)—The SBDC is a university-based center for the delivery of joint government, academic, and private sector services for the benefit of small business and the national welfare which is committed to the development and productivity of business and the economy in specific geographical regions.

SMALL BUSINESS ADMINISTRATION (SBA)—Organization whose fundamental purpose is to aid, counsel, assists and protect the interest of small businesses.

SMALL BUSINESS CORPORATION—A corporation which satisfies the definition of I.R.C. §1371(a), §1244(c)(2) or both. Satisfaction of I.R.C. §1371(a) permits a Subchapter S election, while satisfaction of I.R.C. §1244 enables the shareholders of the corporation to claim an ordinary loss on the worthlessness of the stock.

SMALL BUSINESS INVESTMENT ACT—Federal legislation enacted in 1958 under which investment companies may be organized for supplying long term equity capital to small businesses.

SOLE PROPRIETORSHIP—A form of business in which one person owns all the assets of the business, and is solely liable for the debts of the business.

SPECIFIC PERFORMANCE—The equitable remedy requiring the party who breaches a contract to perform his or her obligations under the contract.

STOCK CERTIFICATE—A certificate issued to a shareholder which evidences partial ownership of the shareholder in a company.

STRICT LIABILITY—A concept applied by the courts in product liability cases, in which a seller is liable for any and all defective or hazardous products which unduly threaten a consumer's personal safety.

SUBLEASE—Transaction whereby tenant grants interests in leased premises less than his own, or reserves a reversionary interest in the term.

SUBSTANTIAL PERFORMANCE—The performance of nearly all of the essential terms of a contract so that the purpose of the contract has been accomplished giving rise to the right to compensation.

SUM CERTAIN—Liquidated damages pursuant to contract, promissory note, law, etc.

TAFT-HARTLEY ACT—Refers to the Labor-Management Relations Act of 1947, which was established to prescribe the legitimate rights of both employees and employers.

TARIFF—A form of tax assessed against imported and exported goods.

TIME IS OF THE ESSENCE—A clause in a contract which states that the specified time of performance is an essential term of the contract which, if breached, will serve to discharge the entire contract.

TRADE ASSOCIATION—An organization established to benefit members of the same trade by informing them of issues and developments within the organization and about how changes outside the organization will affect them.

TRADE CREDIT—Debt arising through credit sales and recorded as an account receivable by the seller and as an account payable by the buyer.

TRADEMARK—Refers to any mark, word, symbol or other device used by a manufacturer to identify its products.

TRUTH IN LENDING ACT—A federal law which requires commercial lenders to provide applicants with detailed, accurate and understandable information relating to the cost of credit, so as to permit the borrower to make an informed decision.

TURNOVER—As it pertains to a business, turnover is the number of times that an average inventory of goods is sold during a fiscal year or some designated period which measures the efficiency of a business.

UNCONSCIONABLE—Refers to a bargain so one-sided as to amount to an absence of meaningful choice on the part of one of the parties, together with terms which are unreasonably favorable to the other party.

UNDELIVERED ORDERS—The amount of orders for goods and services outstanding for which, the liability has not yet accrued.

UNFAIR LABOR PRACTICE—Any activities carried out by either a union or an employer which violate the National Labor Relations Act.

UNIFORM COMMERCIAL CODE (UCC)—The UCC is a code of laws governing commercial transactions which was designed to bring uniformity to the laws of the various states.

UNILATERAL CONTRACT—A contract whereby one party makes a promise to do or refrain from doing something in return for actual performance by the other party.

UNION SHOP—A workplace where all of the employees are members of a union.

USURIOUS CONTRACT—A contract that imposes interest at a rate which exceeds the legally permissible rate.

USURY—Interest which exceeds the legal rate charged to a borrower for the use of money.

VARIANCE—Permission to depart from the literal requirements of a zoning ordinance.

VENDOR—A seller.

VENTURE CAPITAL—Money used to support new or unusual commercial undertakings; equity, risk or speculative capital.

VOLUNTARY ARBITRATION—Arbitration which occurs by mutual and free consent of the parties.

WARRANTY—An assurance by one party to a contract that a certain fact exists and may be relied upon by the other party to the contract.

WARRANTY OF FITNESS FOR A PARTICULAR PURPOSE—A warranty that goods purchased are suitable for the specific purpose of the buyer.

WARRANTY OF MERCHANTABILITY—A warranty that goods purchased are fit for the general purpose for which they are being purchased.

WORKERS' COMPENSATION—A state-mandated form of insurance covering workers injured in job-related accidents.

WORKING CAPITAL—Current assets minus current liabilities.

ZONE OF EMPLOYMENT—The physical area within which injuries to an employee are covered by worker compensation laws.

ZONING—The government regulation of land use.

BIBLIOGRAPHY AND
ADDITIONAL READING

Black's Law Dictionary, Fifth Edition. St. Paul, MN: West Publishing Company, 1979.

Small Business Administration (Date Visited: April 2006) <http://www.sba.gov/>.

Social Security Administration (Date Visited: April 2006) <http://www.ssa.gov/>.

Call For Action (Date Visited: April 2006) <http://www.callforaction.org>.

The Consumer Information Center (Date Visited: April 2006) <http://www.pueblo.gsa.gov>.

The Direct Marketing Association (Date Visited: April 2006) <http://www.the-dma.org>.

The Federal Trade Commission (Date Visited: April 2006) <http://www.ftc.gov>.

Legal Information Institute (Date Visited: April 2006) <http://www.law.cornell.edu/>.

The National Association of Small Business Investment Companies (NASBIC) (Date Visited: April 2006) <http://www.nasbic.org/>.

The National Association of Investment Companies (NAIC) (Date Visited: April 2006) <http://www.naicvc.com/>.

The Society for Human Resources Management (Date Visited: April 2006) <http://www.shrm.org/>.

The United States Department of Justice (Date Visited: April 2006) <http://www.usdoj.gov/>.

The United States Department of Labor (Date Visited: April 2006) <http://www.dol.gov/>.

The United States Environmental Protection Agency (Date Visited: April 2006) <http://www/epa.gov/>.

The United States Equal Opportunity Commission (Date Visited: April 2006) <http://www.eeoc.gov/>.